AI
WISDOM

VOLUME 1

META-PRINCIPLES OF THINKING
AND LEARNING

TIM DASEY, PH.D.

Published in the United States by Rejuvenate Publishing, Rhode Island.

This book was written with the *assistance* of AI, in dozens of different ways. I think it helped improve the product and accelerated the process. It was not written *by* AI, except for specific sections where the AI content is clearly noted, such as when I quote an AI output. I take responsibility for each word. This is nothing close to the book AI would have produced on its own. I was in control of the output, not AI, as I preach.

Paperback ISBN: 979-8-9882386-4-5
Hardcover ISBN: 979-8-9882386-5-2
eBook ISBN: 979-8-9882386-3-8

Dedication

To my children Julia and Rachel who are a constant supply of motivation for my work. They have blossomed into amazing adults. I hope this book helps their future world be a place of nuance, reason, empathy, and personal agency.

To my parents John and Mary, who passed away in 2024. They nurtured my curious mind and never told me what to think.

To Evangelia "Litsa" Micheli-Tzanakou and all the other educators who go beyond content and make a difference in a student's life.

CONTENTS

PROLOGUE

T his is an ambitious book.

I want to boil AI (artificial intelligence) down to its enduring essence because it could be the foundation of next-generation schooling, not just a sideshow.

I want to show that, in many respects, people aren't thinking about AI in the right ways.

I want to make it obvious that teaching the AI essence doesn't require that students use AI or screens.

The essence isn't even technical or mathematical. Educators intimidated by technology, coding, and math won't find the AI essence intimidating.

And I'm audacious enough to think that when you're done reading, you might agree with me, even if you're not a big fan of AI.

The roots of AI are the meta-principles of thinking and learning. As a prefix, meta- refers to something of a higher order. A meta-principle is a more abstracted view that can illuminate the unifying theme of a domain, guiding various applications. I'm not telling you much in the book about the details of AI's thinking and learning. I'm taking you through the strategy and considerations for getting a machine to do so.

AI Wisdom Volume 1 isn't about teaching *with* AI, but rather about teaching *about* the subsurface roots of AI, the aspects that will be a stable, slowly evolving foundation.

The dizzying array of AI methods and products and the pace at which they change can make it seem like nothing can be taught today that is assured of being relevant when students graduate. I want to dispel that notion.

Perhaps it seems the fundamentals are about how to prompt AI—that the skills of communication, collaboration, critical thinking, and creativity once again reign supreme. That seems to be the orientation of AI literacy, manifested in *prompting* instruction. There's nothing wrong with this. I wholeheartedly wish these efforts to expand. You've got to start somewhere. It's just that AI prompting 101 is a veneer—useful for getting started, but not durable. AI products won't look the same or even be functionally similar when the students graduate. If all they have is familiarity with the last generation of products, adjusting to the next change will be difficult.

One issue is that prompting templates are a formulaic view implying there's a secret decoder to unlocking AI's potential. That seems to treat AI as a traditional machine just waiting for our rules of engagement. Instead, people need to think of AI more like a person than a machine.

That's uncomfortable and not entirely accurate. There are many ways people can think and learn that AI doesn't yet. And even with a human-like intelligence, there's little guarantee AI will behave as a human would in many situations.

There are common ways any intelligence must process and learn from information. In those respects, many AI meta-principles are human ones too, though manifested differently in brains than in AI.

For that reason, teaching AI meta-principles doesn't require screens and can be integrated in any subject. Any topic can be an opportunity for discussing how the students are thinking and learning in AI-relevant language, for role-playing AI personas, or for older age groups, using simplified AI.

I'm not discounting the value of AI interaction experience but rather saying I'd rather they know how AI ticks but get no practice applying those notions than use AI without understanding what they're getting into. Understanding AI's durable roots directly affects how you prompt AI. It's still learning from you, so the meta-principles of how it thinks and learns are always useful.

I want students to have durable knowledge and skills (a.k.a. 21st-Century Skills[1]) because AI changes too fast. They need the "laws of physics" for AI, though I chose that phrase because of familiarity. Laws are hard to come by in AI. Concepts and tradeoffs are more realistic.

The rapid emergence of AI has created an urgent need to understand its enduring roots, yet there's a striking gap in educational literature that motivated this book. While many resources address using AI tools, adapting practices, or AI's societal impact, few tackle the fundamental principles that students need to understand about how AI thinks and learns.

My first book, *Wisdom Factories,* argued for a fundamental reimagining of education in response to AI, moving from expertise factories to centers of wisdom development.[2] This volume focuses on understanding AI itself. If *Wisdom Factories* was the compass pointing toward a necessary transformation of education, this book is the terrain map of AI. The compass tells you where to go, but to actually navigate the territory, you need to understand its features.

AI Wisdom provides educators with the foundational knowledge about AI's nature, capabilities, and implications that they'll need to make informed decisions about that journey.

This book, Volume 1, describes those "laws" of thinking, learning, and teaching that necessarily apply to any intelligent entity, us included.

The second book, Volume 2, discusses meta-principles for using AI and analyzing its implications.

To use an analogy, understanding a person helps you leverage their skills most productively (Volume 1), but there must be an approach toward using that person on any specific problem (Volume 2).

I supply many analogies between AI and brains, but they are clearly not equivalent. The distinctions matter. Understanding how AI and people are different supplies critical applied intuition toward managing AI conversations and behaviors.

Yet where AI and brains do overlap is in a rich set of principles about how any intelligence must deal with the world. AI gets to its functionality differently than brains but abstractly motivated by them. It's a bit like comparing airplanes to birds. Engineers got big pieces of metal to fly by giving the machine the ability to go super-fast, not by flapping its wings. Similarly, AI takes aspects of brain architecture and turbo-charges it. Both birds and planes fly, and each handle different desired flight functionalities (getting somewhere fast versus dexterous maneuvering).

I'm about to show you an entirely different way of thinking about AI and what to learn about it.

This is a book for everyone who needs to learn about AI, which is everyone. You may or may not like it, but AI's a big deal, and it's so different from prior technology that uneducated usually means misinformed. There is unfortunately a ton of speculation, red herrings, finger pointing, and anger going around about AI. Most of it is a distraction at best, and a lot is totally wrong.

I'm specifically addressing educators, but teaching doesn't just happen in school. We all teach AI when we use it, and managers, leaders, and parents are educators too.

There's not much reason to believe AI education for the typical student will go below the surface. A huge chunk of U.S. students graduate high school with no computer science courses, 25-ish years after declaring it a priority.[3] In colleges, while math and science are usually part of general education requirements, information and computer science are relatively neglected.

The business world doesn't wait for the education systems, but it's limited by them. If we haven't adapted education to AI's prominence in a fraction of the time of computer science rollout, then I think students are in trouble. Heck, our societies are in trouble. Deep AI understanding requires mindsets and practices that take a lot of time to develop. They are core, like literacy and numeracy. You can't impart those in a quick training.

One of the things you'll learn from this book is modern AI doesn't have techno-stench—the way technical or mathematical jargon often repels non-STEM educators and much of the adult population. I can talk about it in plain language, not specialist language.

It's probably useful to provide a glimpse of where my thinking comes from.

***

I feel my perspective might be unique. I was trained on AI and on people. I wanted to understand how both thought and learned.

It began as an undergraduate electrical and computer engineering major. I started overloading with biology classes halfway through. By the time I thought about graduate school, I wanted both, so I chose biomedical engineering at Rutgers University, beginning in 1986.

My Ph.D. advisor was a middle-aged woman of Greek heritage named Evangelia Micheli-Tzanakou. Everyone called her Litsa. She was tough and tenacious about her lab's work, but I was at times mothered as much as taught. It wasn't overbearing; it was what I needed at that point in my life. That was the greatest gift I got from any educator.

Litsa's own mid-career dissertation studied the visual system of animals, mainly frogs. She had developed a unique way to measure what individual neurons in frog visual systems were recognizing about images.[4] An electrode was placed on an awake frog's neuron to measure the electricity the brain cell produces when the frog was shown a visual pattern.

But what visual pattern? There are a gazillion possible images to show the frog. Whatever images Litsa might pick reflect a potentially biased expectation. Instead, the image that evokes the strongest response should be revealed by the neuron itself.

You couldn't walk up to another person and know the best way to interact with them when you'd never met them. Litsa had the same issue meeting a frog neuron.

There was another complication. The experiment didn't allow many tries. If you stimulate a real neuron too much it accommodates—it gets used to being stimulated and incrementally stops responding as much. You don't get many image attempts before it's hard to tell whether the neuron is tired, or the image is suboptimal.

The way she approached the problem guided my eventual Ph.D. path and AI-infused career. She treated it as an *optimization* problem, something I will talk about a few times in this book. Optimizations are processes that improve something toward its best possible state. Starting with random pixels, she changed each one in each image iteration until the neuron response stopped getting better. The way the image changed was the interesting part. It wasn't a pre-defined path, but rather a way of learning the direction toward a better image.

I played around with lots of optimization methods and eventually optimized ("trained") this new stuff called *artificial neural networks* (or just *neural networks*), the basis of most modern AI. I started making customized neural networks, including one attempt to mimic the functionality of the cells in a human retina. I spent a lot of time trying to understand how changing the learning constraints, methods, or training data affected the learned functionality of the neural networks. Then I applied my dissertation to interpretation of human brain waves for detecting Multiple Sclerosis.[5] My dissertation committee had an engineer, a neuroscientist, and a perceptual psychologist. I've long had an interdisciplinary bent.

My view is also independent from the existing AI education mindset in higher education (Science, Technology, Engineering, and Mathematics) majors. I got little formal education in AI. It was too new when I was learning it. I have skimmed through texts and courses occasionally, but most of what I know is from making AI, being around great AI researchers, and reading research papers, not taking courses. Ditto for most of my neuroscience and psychology knowledge.

I never would have been able to play with AI in graduate school without coding expertise, but even my first exposure to coding was mostly self-taught. I first learned to code in a self-paced, project-only high school class in 1981 on a first-generation personal computer: a Radio Shack TRS-80 with 16K memory and cassette deck storage.

Let me say that again. 1981. Some teacher whose name I can no longer remember launched me down a path that kept me near the leading edge, all because he got ahead of the curve.

In 1982 I went to the first college in the U.S.—Clarkson University—to offer PCs (Zenith Z-100s) to every student. They were about $6,000 in today's dollars, and I couldn't afford one, but my roommates let me share. PCs weren't that thrilling then. You wrote a document, or you coded. We were engineers, so we coded. The school put me in a position to learn simply by giving more access to computers.

By the time Litsa got me, I already had enough years under my belt thinking about the possibilities of computers that I could jump in on the beginnings of *machine learning*—how artificial neural nets are taught. I also learned from researchers around the world, not only from their papers, but from this experimental thing called ARPANET.[6] It was a precursor to the Internet, and loaded with other scientists, not trolls.

A year earlier and I wouldn't have gotten the high school programming course. Had I attended a different undergraduate school or been born a couple of years earlier my coding experience would have been much less. A different choice for graduate school and I would have missed out on Litsa's inspiration, and direct access to other researchers via ARPANET. At that time, only a couple of hundred U.S. colleges were enrolled. Over and over, I was in the right place at the right time.

My ability to follow the field since that time is anchored in the fundamentals I learned long ago, deepened by years of experiential variation. I worked at MIT Lincoln Laboratory, their national security laboratory, for 31 years. I spent ten years developing AI and software for aviation weather challenges, followed by twenty years leading AI-infused research and development groups that tackled problems in disparate fields: biological and chemical defense, law enforcement and security, disaster and pandemic management, medicine and biology, transportation safety and logistics, and homeland security.

What I know is largely self-taught, with a good deal of experiential learning. I was around a lot of really smart people and worked a wide range of AI-related problems. That kind of experience rubs off on anybody.

I think I can offer a unique perspective. I hope it's useful.

***

Before diving in, I have a bit of housekeeping to do.

First a plea. There are many hands-on trailblazers in AI education and in AI use in education. There are also some who are doing innovative teaching and don't use AI at all. I have huge respect for them. They are the engines that make change work, and they need your support. This is not the time to constrain teacher or administrator innovation.

The caution is in thinking that I'm a Silicon Valley mouthpiece trying to push AI down your throats. Where this becomes relevant are the times when I tell you what I *think* will happen. Please avoid the tendency to think it's what I *wish* will happen. I have massive concerns too that have driven me to focus on your students.

A corollary is that I often criticize the education system. That is not a criticism about the individuals in the system, all of whom are captive to it in various ways.

Educational institutions may upload the book into AI conversations. People don't read many books anymore, so deciding to write one requires more pause than it once did. I believe a big value of this book is putting AI into the appropriate mindset to help you generate customized curricula.

However, I'm not interested in handing the work to AI companies for training their models, nor does this permission extend to uses for other for-profit product developments. That means you have a responsibility to make sure your account settings don't allow use of your conversations for model retraining.

Most of the time, when I say "AI," I'm referring to *AI Large Language Models (LLMs)* that we talk or text with. It's one form of *Generative AI (GenAI)* that creates information instead of just analyzing it. There are many other forms of AI. It gets tiresome to add specificity to every AI reference, so I will only add more specific terms when the assumption of it being a GenAI language model is invalid or incomplete.

Whether our society makes the right decisions about AI, or anything else, is highly dependent on whether your students can learn to make effective, nuanced judgments on complex matters. The solution isn't as simple as an AI prompting class, but it's far more valuable—AI or not—because it gets at the heart of the most important skills in modern life.

AI doesn't have to be scary. I'm betting by the end of the book you'll wonder why you weren't teaching this stuff to every student all along. Because effectively using AI tools depends on understanding AI's roots.

INTRODUCTION

M any educators view AI through familiar lenses that ultimately mislead.

Some see AI as just another tech tool to master, like interactive whiteboards or learning management systems. But AI proficiency isn't about learning software features. AI proficiency is about knowing how to express your needs, situations, intents, and values, iterate and tinker toward shared understanding, and have the sense to reframe the way you work or live, if desired, so AI can help more. You aren't going to become skilled at AI interaction because you learned the product features in a training class.

Others dismiss it as too complex for non-specialists to understand. They still see a bright line between STEM and what they do, but that line has eroded. The innards of AI are very technical and mathematical, yet its concepts can be explained in digestible ways. Few people understand the details of neuroscience either, but they can easily listen to a psychology podcast. By abstracting core principles from technical details, the knowledge becomes more actionable.

In the case of AI, the fundamentals have two aspects.

This book, Volume 1, explores the meta-principles of intelligence and adaptation, of thinking and learning. The cool synergy is that these fundamentals apply to brains, organizations, and societies too, though expressed through different mechanisms. Knowing how AI thinks and learns will inform how you interact with it, as with a person.

1

Volume 2 addresses the meta-considerations of using AI, such as common uses for AI-human combinations, emerging topics like AI "reasoning," agents, and teams, and the mentalities needed to use AI safely and ethically.

Together, these books teach about AI, but also intelligence more broadly. Since these ideas apply to any subject, they offer the all-of-curriculum glue that's been missing in teaching durable skills like critical thinking, creativity, and interpersonal skills.

This book challenges our assumptions about intelligence itself.

AI IS NOT A BRAIN, BUT SHARES SOME PRINCIPLES

The brain has been a crucial inspiration for AI development, particularly over the past forty years. Early pioneers like John Hopfield and Geoffrey Hinton, who shared the 2024 Nobel Prize in Physics,[7] drew from neuroscience to create artificial neural networks that can learn from experience.

Today, neural networks are standard in AI. They often incorporate principles first understood through studying the brain.[8,9] Neuroscience aspects are selectively and knowingly incorporated into AI. The most innovative advances have frequently come from scientists who actively study both artificial and natural intelligence.

But less reported is the effect AI has had on teaching us how brains work.[10,11,12,13] Brains and AI have to deal with the "information problem", as Peter Robin Hiesinger explained in his 2022 book *The Self-Assembling Brain*.[14] They both face the challenge of requiring more information to specify their final state (what they know, understand, and can do) than is contained in their initial state (genetic code for brains, training data and parameters for AI). Therefore, both systems must rely on self-organization.

While both AI and the brain can be black boxes whose mechanisms are opaque, AI systems are easier to study because every connection and component is known by the AI creator. Specially constructed AI models, often with more biological realism, have helped neuroscientists better understand brain functions, target experiments more effectively, and propose new theories of brain operation. Neuroscientist researchers have even adopted some AI terminology.

AI and the brain share some fundamental principles of thinking and learning but differ in important ways. Rather than trying to perfectly copy the brain, AI developers experiment with different aspects of brain-like processing to discover what's essential for intelligence. Understanding these high-level principles of how intelligence works is key to both using AI effectively and developing our own cognitive abilities.

This doesn't mean teaching the nitty gritty of neuroscience and brain architecture, which is interesting knowledge but not that actionable in conversations with modern AI. Rather, high-level heuristics about brains, AI, and information itself are the impactful principles.

Such insights are often applied and even learned unconsciously. That's why the book is called *AI Wisdom*, with strong allusion to intuition. Our unconscious makes most of our decisions, not our frontal lobe. A high-altitude view of education reform, motivated by AI, was expressed in my 2023 book, *Wisdom Factories*.[15] In it I talk about the importance of educating intuitions, not just the conscious brain. Intuition is the manifestation of much of wisdom.

Whereas *Wisdom Factories* was very high level, maybe so much that oxygen masks are needed, *AI Wisdom* gets at what that philosophy really means. It means focusing on *meta-principles*.

But what meta-principles?

EDUCATOR, MEET AI

The question of "what is AI?" has always perplexed me, but especially so in the GenAI era of ChatGPT, Claude, Gemini, Llama, DeepSeek, Mistral, Grok, and a constantly evolving cast of smaller AI players.

It's not that I don't know the answer; I know several answers. I'm perplexed when asked because I'm trying to figure out what question they really want me to answer. Are they asking how AI works under the hood? Are they asking how AI will impact the world? Do they want to know what it means for education? The "what" question has many answers.

I see it as a broader plea for understanding. In that respect, it's a good question, one any learner should ask. It's general enough that the questioner can supply an interpretation, not just a definition.

I've reframed the question for both Volume 1 and 2 to "What about AI is different than prior innovations?" Aspects of that answer are given by each chapter.

In Part I (Metacognition), I discuss how AI processes information. Chapter 1, "Pattern Analyzing," reveals how AI recognizes complex patterns through vast networks of simple units, showing how sophisticated capabilities emerge from many basic elements working together. Chapter 2, "Transforming," examines how AI converts information between different forms, from categorizing and measuring to ranking and reimagining. Chapter 3,

"Knowing," tackles whether the terms we apply to people's thinking really apply to AI. Chapter 4, "Conceptual," examines how AI operates primarily through statistical patterns rather than facts. Chapter 5, "Creative," examines how AI's conceptual nature enables creative capabilities that can rival human creativity, forcing us to reconsider what makes human creativity special.

Part II, Meta-Learning and Teaching, examines how AI develops its capabilities. Chapter 6, "Learning," explores the fundamental mechanisms behind AI learning, revealing surprising parallels with human education. Chapter 7, "Adaptive," examines how AI handles changing environments and evolving goals. Chapter 8, "Data-Driven," investigates how the examples we show AI shape its understanding and behavior. Chapter 9, "Erring," confronts AI's mistakes and biases, exploring why they occur and how to manage them.

The final chapters tie the lessons together and look forward.

Chapter 10 outlines the key ingredients for teaching these meta-principles effectively: complex, open-ended challenges; student agency; learning through experience and productive struggle; building understanding across domains; and structured reflection and iteration. Rather than prescribing a specific curriculum, I provide examples of how to integrate these principles across different contexts.

Chapter 11, "What's Next?" examines how AI capabilities continue to evolve, exploring the implications of increasingly sophisticated AI systems and why understanding these fundamental principles will only become more crucial. It previews Volume 2's focus on how to effectively direct and integrate AI capabilities.

BACKDROP, NOT BLUEPRINT

I could have written a curriculum, but I didn't think the mass audience was ready for that without a lot of explanation. We're in a unique position—starting with a blank slate but constrained by the limited time we've had to reflect on AI since ChatGPT's introduction.

Another challenge in writing a curriculum now is that integration will vary across schools and classrooms. One school might want an AI course requirement. Another might integrate it into each subject, like Computational Thinking does for software-related meta-skills. Others might take a plunge into wholesale adoption. Every curriculum framework must adapt to its unique context. Choosing one path means a suboptimal fit for other contexts. I don't want to make those choices for you but rather arm you with the knowledge to make your own.

At the end of each chapter, I have outlined the meta-principles addressed in the chapter and provided rough examples of how it could manifest at age levels from elementary school through college. They're just examples. Thinking and learning hopefully happen in every lesson! Often class lessons are about other people that have thought and learned. The AI meta-principles fit in any lesson, at a minimum as a contrast to human thinking and learning.

Shifting perspectives on intelligence and learning requires repeated exposure across varied contexts. These mindset changes won't stick after a single lesson or unit. While dedicated AI courses may sometimes be needed, the core concepts this book describes are best woven throughout existing subjects. A biology teacher exploring how simple cell interactions create complex organisms is teaching the same *distributed processing* principles that underlie AI. An economics teacher examining how markets respond to change is teaching the same adaptation principles we see in some AI learning.

Integrating AI across subjects serves multiple purposes. It helps students see recurring principles across disciplines. It demonstrates that these aren't just AI concepts but rather fundamental principles about how intelligence processes information and learns from experience.

We need everyone's creativity to figure out the path forward. My goal is simply to open your eyes to learning opportunities far beyond prompting.

***

This flexible approach to implementation reflects the diverse perspectives educators bring to AI education. I'm triangulating different educator camps.

For educators who buy into using AI in their teaching and are ready to move beyond basic AI literacy, I'm offering deeper foundations that will endure future AI advances.

I also address those with deep reservations about AI's impact on academic integrity, student development, society, or global affairs. I show that neither they nor their students need to use AI to teach or learn about it. Students can benefit from experimentation with AI in higher grade levels, but often those can be small AI models for specific educational purposes, not giant, GenAI models like ChatGPT. This does not mean experience with GenAI is unimportant. GenAI use is essential for developing the highest competencies. Some Volume 2 topics require GenAI use, but most of Volume 1 can be taught without it.

For the rest who aren't sure what to think about AI, I'm offering a carrot. Making explicit how we and AI think and learn is incredibly valuable. Whether you embrace or question AI in education, the *AI Wisdom* meta-principles can support the development of durable skills.

The aim is to provide foundational understanding that can inform many different educational paths rather than espouse a prescription. Whether you're designing AI-enhanced curriculum, seeking AI-free approaches to modern skills development, or simply trying to understand what's truly important about AI beyond the headlines, these principles offer valuable perspectives.

It's not a liberal arts world now just because we can talk to GenAI. As AI developers, we are problem solvers—an inherently STEM-oriented skill. And the fact that judgment about using AI requires knowledge of our own strengths and weaknesses reveals a need for the humanities too. Everyone will need management and leadership skills to navigate AI agents and teams. The business community knows entirely new models of companies, skills, and entire industries are likely.

The work world has long been trending multidisciplinary. Interacting with AI inherently requires a multidisciplinary approach. Every educator has a role to play.

PART I. METACOGNITION

C an you write down your rules for predicting whether it's going to rain? Without looking at your weather app I mean. Maybe you notice the feeling in the air, the color of the clouds, the smells, the birds' behavior, or a subtle shift in the wind. Together these clues form a pattern that your brain processes mostly unconsciously. That's what I mean by intuition, and robust intuition is the basis of wisdom.

Trying to write rules for intuition feels preposterous—and the same is true for AI.

The most transformative AI systems differ fundamentally from traditional computer technology. Traditional computer programs follow precise instructions: "if X happens, do Y." But AI, like your brain, works through patterns and concepts and complex webs of relationships that can't be reduced to simple rules.

AI is still created in software, but in two pieces that are very different from traditional computer programs. The first is training software, whose instructions describe a process for teaching the AI. Teaching AI is the subject of Part II.

The second piece—the inference engine—applies the trained AI model to new information. However, that program just executes the math in the AI neural network. Translating that math—configured indirectly by training—into an explanation of AI's decisions remains a major research challenge. Even if you examined the code running a neural network, you wouldn't truly understand what it's doing.

The first part of this book challenges fundamental assumptions about intelligence and thinking. AI operates through vast networks that recognize and transform patterns—more like a brain, ant hill, or society than a traditional computer.

The chapters in Part I explore how AI recognizes complex patterns through interconnected networks, transforms information between different representations, builds knowledge through statistical patterns rather than isolated facts, and achieves creative capabilities that aren't supposed to come from machines. Along the way, I'll address persistent misconceptions about AI that often keep educators from seeing its true nature.

These principles serve multiple purposes. They shape how you think about AI, helping you harness its strengths and guard against its weaknesses. AI is a sophisticated pattern analyzer that thinks in *concepts* rather than facts or rules. This understanding helps you anticipate when it will prove reliable, when concepts might become confused, and how to guide it toward your desired transformations. Recognizing AI's nature clarifies why it's better suited for ideation than as a mere trivia machine.

But little in these chapters applies only to AI. Extraordinary things emerge when vast networks of simple elements work together. That's useful for understanding organizations, economies, and societies too. And every form of intelligence—whether biological or artificial—must perform certain essential functions to make sense of the world.

1.

PATTERN ANALYZING

Mrs. Chen could tell within seconds of walking into her fourth-grade classroom that something felt off. Maybe it was the unusual quiet, the way Marcus and Jessica avoided each other, or the clusters of students whispering. Without conscious thought, she knew something was different, and quickly adjusted her plans for the class.

Ask Mrs. Chen how she knew, and she'd probably shrug and say, "teacher instinct." But that instinct represents an incredibly sophisticated form of pattern recognition, one that draws on countless subtle cues and years of experience to read a classroom's emotional temperature in an instant.

She's processing many subtle signals simultaneously—body language, sound levels, social groupings, facial expressions—without consciously breaking them down into rules. Her brain has learned these patterns naturally through years of teaching experience, much like how we learn to recognize faces or understand speech without being able to explain exactly how we do it.

For decades, computer scientists dreamed of building AI that could match this kind of intuitive pattern recognition. But they were divided on how to get there. One camp believed the path forward was to break down expert knowledge into clear, logical rules like "if students are unusually quiet, and small groups are whispering, then there's likely social conflict." The other camp, led by researchers like John Hopfield and Geoffrey Hinton, took inspiration from how our brains work. They developed networks of simple units that learn to recognize complex patterns through experience.

Hinton, Hopfield, and their fellow neural network pioneers spent decades pursuing this approach, even as much of the AI community dismissed it as impractical. Conventional wisdom held that computers should solve problems through explicit logical rules—not by detecting patterns in ways we couldn't fully explain. Why create a black-box AI that reached answers through untraceable pathways?

But Hopfield, Hinton, and others saw something the rule-based advocates missed. The most sophisticated human abilities—from reading a room's emotional dynamics to recognizing a face in a crowd—don't rely on explicit rules. They emerge from the brain's ability to learn patterns from experience. This insight would eventually revolutionize AI, though it would take decades for computing power and data availability to catch up with the theory.

Neural networks dominate modern AI. They are mathematical analogs to connected biological neurons. They're the system architecture, the design of the AI.

For students outside computer science, the details of neural net structure are less critical. It satisfies curiosity but offers little broader insight.

However, the meta-principles behind neural networks are crucial. Neural nets:

- Recognize patterns too complex and subtle for rule-based systems
- Use networks of simple elements to handle complex tasks
- Respond to pattern cues rather than direct commands

Networked processing shows up several times in the book series, especially in Volume 2 when I describe AI teams and, believe it or not, societies. *Distributed processing* is everywhere—ant hills, ecosystems, economies, societies, even future AI teams. All those systems recognize and process patterns, even though their units are not neurons but cells, entire minds, or organizations. Studying distributed systems can help learners connect familiar concepts to AI's deeper mysteries.

THE LIMITATIONS OF RULES

Early AI research focused on designing and codifying rule sets for specific areas of human expertise. This involved fusing symbolic language, numerical data, and logical operators into rules to define decision-making processes. These *expert systems* got to be quite complicated. For example, the MYCIN expert system was developed at Stanford University in the 1970s to help diagnose blood infections and recommend the proper antibiotic treatment.[16] It relied on about 600 rules and, in some studies, performed comparably to human experts—but it was rarely used in practice.[17] It would take doctors thirty minutes to enter patient information into MYCIN, the software didn't integrate with clinical workflows, and physicians weren't happy with its explanations.

Eventually expert systems were abandoned due to bigger issues. They were a pain to maintain, like trying to manage a thousand-page teacher's manual, where changing one rule might require updates to hundreds of others. Minor changes in input quality or unexpected situations could cause the entire system to break down. It was simply too brittle, too inflexible.

But the biggest problems with rule-based systems had no cure. Just as no list of rules can capture how Mrs. Chen reads her classroom's dynamics, many important patterns can't be determined very accurately by rules.

Take the ability to recognizing someone based on their appearance. What are your rules for doing that? I know—it's intuitive. But if you had to write down rules, do you think you could get a rule list that does well at recognizing people regardless of who it's supposed to recognize? I couldn't. And if I did, I know the rules would be so full of qualitative factors (what are the limits of broad noses or large eyes?) that all I would have done is break the entire appearance recognition problem into separate rules that remain hard to evaluate.

You can see the difficulty experts have in describing what they do by the "it depends" reaction. I've spent a lot of time watching well-meaning scientists ask operators how they do their jobs. Scientists want to understand better so they can anticipate how technology might fit in. If the technology is AI, then they want to understand the human decisions and processes.

So they ask them how they make decisions.

Crickets ... then ... "it depends."

No expert can write their expertise down in a set of rules. If they're lucky, they can express some of their intuition via heuristics and principles. But that doesn't mean it can be translated easily into rules.

Rule-based AI systems are now rare. If a rule set is simple enough, people either don't need a machine, or conventional software can handle it. If a complex rule set is needed, then inevitably it will fail in many situations.

Hopfield, Hinton and others in the neural network community were taking a completely different approach.

ARTIFICIAL NEURAL NETWORKS

Neural networks take a different approach from rule-based systems, one inspired by how brains are organized and learn.

Artificial neural networks gain their power from combining many simple processing units. The basic building block is an artificial neuron, a simple mathematical unit that's very loosely inspired by brain cells. Each artificial neuron processes multiple inputs, weighting them by connection strength before summing them.

Crucially, the artificial neuron then transforms this sum through a nonlinear function, the *activation function*. Nonlinear means the plot of output versus the summed, weighted inputs isn't a straight line.

That's critical to AI's abilities. Most real-world phenomena aren't straight lines. Weather, image attributes, emotions in prose—almost everything fluctuates. Sometimes there are really sharp edges in information, like in images. With activation functions the AI can fit very complex concepts and relationships. Without that nonlinear piece, neural networks would be stuck thinking in straight lines, unable to capture the rich complexity of its experiences.

Artificial neurons perform simple mathematical operations a middle schooler could do. When you put these basic units together in large numbers, that's when the magic happens.

The collection of connection strengths (a.k.a. weights or hyperparameters) across the neural net is what is taught during neural net training. That's the secret sauce—a bunch of numbers. The largest AI model networks might have billions of these artificial neurons and even more connections between them. I'll get into how the training of those numbers is done in Part II. This part focuses on what it does after being trained.

Most neural network architectures organize their neurons in layers, with information flowing in one direction, as illustrated in Figure 1. If there are a lot of layers, it's called a *deep neural network (DNN)*.

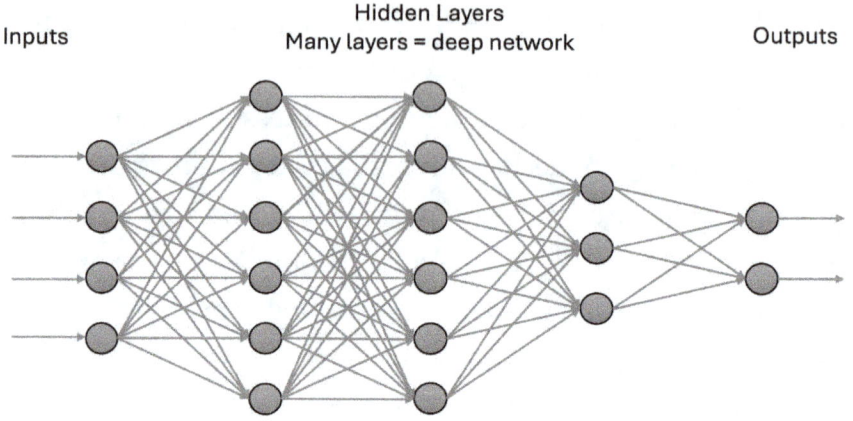

Inputs   **Hidden Layers**
Many layers = deep network   Outputs

Figure 1. Architecture of a typical artificial neural network.[18]

Only when many neurons work together across multiple layers can the network recognize complex patterns. Each subsequent layer builds on what came before, combining these signals in increasingly sophisticated ways. Figure 2 shows the responses of some artificial neurons at different layers in a face recognition neural net hierarchy. Edges in intensity and color are a rich source of information in most images, and those basics are handled at the lowest layers. Those features are combined to analyze face parts in the middle layers, and neurons in the last layers examine entire faces in different ways.

There is a similar progression from simple features to complex aspects in AI language models like ChatGPT.[19,20] Early layers handle syntactic structures and contextual disambiguation. Middle layers address integrative features that might require literacy and linguistics experts to decipher. The deepest (latest) layers analyze wholistic aspects, such as abstract semantic processing, style adaptation, discourse-level features, and emotion recognition. In analyzing writing, for example, early layers might learn to recognize basic grammar patterns, middle layers might identify argument structure, and later layers could assess overall writing quality.

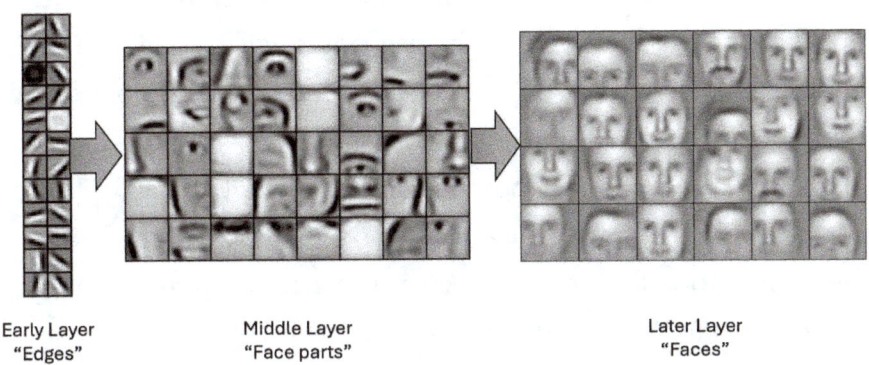

Early Layer
"Edges"

Middle Layer
"Face parts"

Later Layer
"Faces"

Figure 2. Positive (light) and negative (dark) sensitivities to input pixels for artificial neurons at three levels of a face-recognition neural network.[21]

The power of neural nets comes from putting simple math pieces together in large numbers. If someone asks you how AI works, that's the core answer. That revelation doesn't tell you very much though, any more than telling you a brain is comprised of neurons.

Still, I find it wondrous that putting a bunch of simple things together elicits such incredible abilities.

Those who want a deeper dive can get it from the next section, but you won't get lost if you skip it. That's true of all the book sections labeled "Optional."

INSIDE AI INFORMATION (OPTIONAL)

Neural networks have evolved dramatically since their early days, with many evolutions that profoundly impact their capabilities.

The architectures of the 1980s and 1990s were relatively simple, consisting of just a few layers, but researchers recognized early on that larger networks held immense potential. In the late 1980s, researchers proved that a three-layer network could approximate any continuous function, though it might require an enormous number of hidden neurons.[22] It was theorized in the 1990s that multiple layers would be more efficient than a single hidden layer,[23] but it wasn't until the early 2000s that sufficient computing power and training data became available to test these theories.

The way neurons process information has been refined over time, particularly in the choice of activation functions.[24] Most networks employ S-shaped activation functions, which start flat, rise smoothly in the middle, and level off again. Specialized functions like Gaussians have found specific applications where detecting optimal ranges is crucial, though they're less common in modern networks. A major advancement was the introduction of layer-wide activation functions, particularly softmax, which relates to neuronal competition in the brain's cortex.[25] The softmax function creates contrast in neural signals, much like how the loudest voice in a room naturally quiets others, and has become ubiquitous in AI networks, especially in their final layers.

Several key architectural innovations have shaped modern AI. Convolutional Neural Networks (CNNs), pioneered by Yann LeCun (Meta's AI lead) for handwriting recognition, revolutionized how networks process visual information.[26] Rather than connecting each neuron to every input, CNNs apply shared neurons repeatedly to input snippets, reducing connection weights while preserving spatial relationships. This approach proved remarkably versatile, extending beyond vision to any data with meaningful spatial or time-related structure. In audio processing, these filters slide along the time dimension to detect acoustic patterns, while in signal analysis they can identify specific waveform features. The efficiency comes from their ability to detect similar patterns anywhere in the input, whether it's identifying a cat's whiskers in any part of an image or a particular phoneme in a speech signal.

The challenge of processing sequential information was addressed by Long Short-Term Memory (LSTM) networks in 1997.[27] These networks tackled how to handle important information that appears much earlier in a sequence. Standard neural networks struggled with this, essentially trying to understand long sentences while only remembering the last word. LSTMs redesigned the artificial neuron itself so that it's like tiny data processing units with a conveyor belt of information and three learned gates controlling that flow. The forget gate learns what old information to erase, the input gate decides what new information to add, and the output gate controls what gets passed on to the next cell. While more complex than standard neurons, these cells could still be trained through normal neural network methods.

Another breakthrough came with Generative Adversarial Networks (GANs) in 2014, the most prominent early GenAI method, focused on image generation.[28] Like an art forger and detective locked in an endless duel, GANs pit two neural networks against each other: a generator creating fake content and a discriminator trying to spot the fakes. This adversarial process led to dramatic improvements in AI's ability to generate realistic images, demonstrating that AI could create, not just analyze.

And then there was the publication of the transformer architecture in 2017 from Google Research, which revolutionized language processing, and was the original basis behind LLMs.[29] Unlike previous sequential approaches, transformers can dynamically focus on relevant context using an attention mechanism. When processing a word like "bank," the network can focus attention on nearby words to determine if it's referring to a financial institution or a riverside. Modern versions scale efficiently using sparse attention techniques, allowing words to focus on local content while maintaining gist-level awareness of distant content.[30]

The original 2017 transformer paper introduced an encoder-decoder architecture designed for translation (where input text in one language is encoded and then decoded into another language). Current day LLMs usually use a simplified decoder-only design. It's like the difference between a translator (encoder-decoder) and a writer (decoder-only). The writer just needs to generate what comes next based on what they've written so far, while a translator needs to understand the full input sentence before producing any output. This decoder-only approach turned out to be remarkably powerful for general language tasks when scaled up with enough parameters and training data.

These architectural approaches haven't completely replaced each other but rather found their optimal applications in the modern AI landscape. LSTMs continue to excel in processing sensor data and time series where information needs to be processed sequentially, such as in manufacturing quality control or music generation. GANs maintain their value for specific image tasks requiring high visual fidelity, though they've been increasingly replaced by newer approaches like diffusion models for general image generation.[31] The field accumulates these useful architectural tools, with each finding its proper place in the AI ecosystem, demonstrating that innovation in neural network architecture is often not about replacement but about expanding the toolkit available to AI developers.

NETWORK MEMORY

But how do neural nets, or brains, or economies, store information?

To answer that, I need to nudge how you think of memory.

There is a tendency to think of memory as a tangible thing. We talk about it as such. We *lose* memories. We forget a *piece* of information.

In the information world, memory is a much more versatile concept, not limited to individual data items.

Brains have exemplified that for a very long time, but the architectures of conventional computing, with chips that hold specific pieces of information in buckets at known addresses, is more salient to most adults than brain architecture.

The concept of memory is broad. A light switch has memory. It has two states: on and off. Each state can be repeatedly retrieved by a consistent action (flipping the switch up or down). It stores one bit of information. A tree adds rings to its trunk each year, creating a permanent record of its growth patterns. Meta-alloys, when bent out of shape, will "remember" their original form when heated.[32] These shape memory materials find uses from spacecraft to orthodontic braces. Our own bodies hold memories, beyond that of our brains. The immune system remembers pathogens it has encountered before, allowing for a faster, stronger response to repeat infections.[33]

All forms of memory:

- Retain information about past states or events
- Encode information into storable forms
- Retrieve or express stored information when needed

That's it. Memories are stored in an encoded form and are somehow usable later under particular conditions.

In conventional computers, each piece of information is isolated, stored in a specific location, and retrieved by address. Computation and memory are distinct. This architecture treats memory as a collection of separate buckets, each holding a piece of data without inherent meaning or context. The software determines how to interpret and manipulate this data, but the storage itself remains passive.

Early brain researchers were influenced by this compartmentalized view. They debated the idea of a "grandmother cell"—a single neuron that would activate only in response to a highly specific, familiar stimulus, like the sight of one's grandmother.[34] (Ironically, the neuroscientist who first coined the term—Jerry Lettvin—was on my Ph.D. dissertation defense committee.) This concept implied that brain memories might be stored in isolated, discrete units: one cell, one memory. Neuroscientists searched for such cells, hoping to pinpoint neurons tied to specific people, objects, or experiences. Over time, however, research has revealed a much more complex reality.

Memory and recognition aren't confined to individual cells but are distributed across neural networks. Recognition of something as personal as a grandmother involves patterns of activity across many cells, where individual neurons contribute to multiple memories.

This distributed approach enables the brain to recall vast amounts of information without relying on fragile, isolated units that could easily die. As each word contributes a tiny piece to the overall plotline of a book, each neuron has a small role. Think of it as a mosaic. No single tile tells the whole picture, but together they create something much richer.

Neural networks in AI mimic the brain's distributed approach. Instead of storing each piece of information in a separate bucket, they encode memories in patterns across a web of connections, allowing for robustness and flexibility in memory retrieval. The network inherently encodes context too—the relationship between neurons—which the combination of data and software on a conventional computer might never reveal.

It's not just old-time neuroscientists who didn't understand networked memory in the brain. The notion takes quite a while to get used to.

The way AI networks store and retrieve information isn't just an academic detail. It's pretty central to conceptualizing complex systems more generally, and it can assist how we interact with AI. When we provide context or examples to AI, we're activating certain patterns across its network. Understanding this helps explain why AI can seem brilliant in some contexts but struggle with seemingly simple tasks in others. When we construct and manage AI teams and agents, the same principles of networked memory are relevant.

AI doesn't run efficiently on conventional computer processors (CPUs). There's too much time spent getting the data to the processing. Graphics Processing Units (GPUs), so named because they were invented to power computer graphics, contain a bunch of separate processors that have memory and processing together, the way AI needs it, and can process in parallel. Advanced GPUs are critical in training and running AI neural nets. The current GPU supply limitations have made getting them, along with AI engineering talent, the AI industry equivalent of *Survivor*.

Just as neural networks excel through distributed processing, human systems, such as schools and economies, similarly derive power from interconnected networks.

DISTRIBUTED PATTERNS

I would venture that most adults believe that the more neurons activate, the better the thinking. Sci-fi often portrays increased brain activation as a source of extraordinary power. Educators have told me forms of this theory.

There are times when a huge number of brain neurons are firing at once. Epileptic seizures. High-voltage electric shocks. Those are not great times for a brain! There's even a condition called status epilepticus where prolonged seizures can lead to brain damage.[35] All the neurons firing at once creates more heat than the brain can dissipate, damaging itself.

This view assumes that cognitive power is simply a matter of volume, but effective thinking and memory rely on the specific patterns of activation across a network of cells. The brain stores information not in isolated cells or by lighting up as many cells as possible, but in complex, distributed patterns where the arrangement and connections between neurons encode meaning.

Memories overlap in networks, with parts of each pattern relevant to multiple memories. That means flooding the brain with widespread activation can lead to interference rather than clarity, as it disrupts the subtle differences needed to distinguish one memory or concept from another.

Distributed knowledge shows up outside of AI and brain neural networks too. Knowledge in a culture is spread across countless individuals, each carrying fragments of stories, skills, or values. No single individual has all the knowledge, but the collective creates the full picture of that society's customs and understandings. Ditto for an economies, social networks, and organizations like schools.

A neural network does not store isolated facts in specific neurons, real or artificial. Instead, it stores relationships and patterns that are distributed across the network. This is how both brains and AI can be so powerful—because they don't depend on perfect, orderly storage, which necessarily requires choices about organization schemes.

Those of you who organize filing systems will understand. There's no perfect system. Organize by customer and you'll have a hard time finding the information when the need is by product line instead. Distributed storage doesn't have to make that choice. The whole culture is stored in a human network and their artifacts. Similarly, a neural net doesn't have to pick a filing system. It can file in lots of ways by the pattern of connections across simple units. Folders don't allow that nuance.

The distributed nature of this knowledge, however, is what makes understanding what's happening inside the AI black box so difficult. Each artificial neuron in an AI neural network contributes to a small part of the output; its real behavior emerges only through the interactions across the entire network.

Neural networks have an astonishing ability to store and recognize countless patterns within the same architecture, but there's a capacity limit. At some point the network patterns overlap too much, and memories can interfere.

Network memory has a much different degradation mechanism. Lose a conventional computer's memory and it's gone entirely. Lose a few neurons out of the network and most of the memory patterns are still preserved. My analogy is to taking care of a lawn. Neglect it a bit and the lawn doesn't go away immediately, but grass is replaced slowly with undesirable weeds. In the case of brains (but not AI), every time we recall a memory, it gets restored according to how our brain currently thinks of it.[36] The brain does some mowing and weed killing. If not for this mechanism, memories of childhood would still be from our childhood mind's point of view, rather than an adult brain that recast the experience.

DISTRIBUTED PATTERN PROCESSORS IN HUMAN SYSTEMS

Long before computers, humans developed various systems for processing information and patterns beyond individual capability. These distributed systems, where multiple components work together to process information, are everywhere once you start looking for them, and they are "intelligent." Some are formal and explicitly designed, like markets and bureaucracies.[37] Others emerge more organically through social interaction.[38]

Like modern AI, they work by reducing complex realities into standardized patterns that can be processed at scale.[39]

Consider how social norms work: they process complex social situations into acceptable and unacceptable behaviors without anyone explicitly programming these rules.[40] What's considered polite or rude in a culture emerges from countless interactions, with the collective system "recognizing" patterns of behavior that work or don't work for that society. No individual designs these norms, yet they effectively process social information at massive scale.

Professional roles similarly emerge to handle complexity.[41] The patterns of behavior we associate with teacher, doctor, or manager weren't centrally designed but evolved as distributed solutions to recurring social needs. These roles process complex social situations into standardized responses, much like how AI transforms complex inputs into standardized outputs.

When a school district identifies and responds to emerging student needs, it often works like a distributed network. Individual teachers notice subtle patterns in student behavior or learning that might not show up in traditional metrics. These observations spread through informal teacher networks, creating a collective recognition of trends that no single data point or rule could capture. For instance, teachers might collectively notice shifts in student engagement patterns across different subjects and teaching styles, leading to organic adjustments in teaching approaches before any formal policy changes.

This is different from analyzing test scores or attendance data with traditional statistics. Instead, it's more like Mrs. Chen's classroom intuition scaled up through networks of educators, where the pattern recognition emerges from many connected observations and adaptations rather than from analyzing centralized data.

This happens in various subnets that are more tightly connected, and at various scales. Students form social networks that develop sophisticated behavioral patterns. Teacher networks collectively recognize effective practices and emerging student needs. Parent networks identify and respond to trends. These networks operate and interact across classroom, school, district, and national scales, each level emerging from simpler interactions but creating capabilities beyond what individuals could achieve. Like other networked systems, they process information through distributed recognition rather than centralized control.

Markets detect patterns through price signals.[42] When millions of individual buying and selling decisions get reduced to price movements, the market is essentially performing distributed pattern recognition across vast amounts of information about supply, demand, and value. No individual participant needs to understand all the factors affecting oil prices or housing costs; the distributed system processes that complexity into actionable signals.

Bureaucracies similarly transform complex realities into standard forms and categories that can be processed systematically.[43] When you fill out a government form or medical chart, you're feeding information into a distributed processing system that, like AI, needs standardized inputs to recognize patterns. A social services bureaucracy, for example, must somehow process millions of unique human situations into actionable categories. That kind of pattern recognition would overwhelm any individual human mind.

Historically, both markets and bureaucracies faced similar criticisms to those now leveled at AI: they were seen as alien and dehumanizing because they reduce rich realities to simplified patterns.[44] Yet over time, we've come to accept them as essential tools for handling complexity beyond individual human scale. They remind us that distributed pattern recognition isn't unique to AI.

When we see AI as part of this longer history of distributed information processing systems, some of its apparent mysteries become clearer.[45]

But I've been skipping over something important. Remember my shorthand explanation of memory as "stored in an encoded form and are somehow usable later under particular conditions?" How exactly are these network patterns made usable?

PATTERNED CUES

It's easy to define how to unlock a memory in a conventional computer. You have a line of code go retrieve the memory. If you have the address, then you can get the memory.

Retrieving an AI or brain memory is similar, except the address isn't simple. It's a pattern too. Cognitive researchers often refer to inputs that trigger certain memories as "cues", so I'll call them *patterned cues*. Some brain scientists call the cue pattern a "semantic pointer."[46]

In the case of LLMs, these patterned cues are simply words or phrases from your prompts that put the network into a certain state.

AI models adapt responses based on subtle variations in input cues. Consider the following prompts I entered into ChatGPT-4 in 2023 and their results:

- "Twinkle twinkle little star" provides the history of the lullaby.
- "Twinkle twinkle little star…" completes the lyrics.
- "Write creatively. Twinkle twinkle little star" produces a story about Twinkleton the star.
- "Act as a scientist. Twinkle twinkle little star" explains the physics of star twinkling.
- "Act as a professor of ancient history. Twinkle twinkle little star" describes stars' role in ancient navigation.

Prompts act as pattern cues, guiding which of the artificial neurons activate to retrieve task-relevant information.

The cues can be subtle. Just as we humans can pick up nuances— whether someone is being sarcastic or sincere, for instance—AI language models are sensitive to subtleties within language. The phrasing of a question, the tone, or even a single word can trigger an entirely different response. The AI has stored a wide variety of concepts and recognizes which ones to bring to the fore based on the way the user interacts with it.

This makes AI language models incredibly versatile. Instead of training a different model for each task (like storytelling, solving math problems, or holding a debate), they use the same network for all these purposes. Whether the AI is useful to us is all about the pattern cues we use to unlock the knowledge hidden inside, and of course whether the AI was trained to have that knowledge to begin with. The reason most GenAI can respond to such a wide range of queries is not that they have a separate module for each topic but that these different knowledge patterns are distributed across the same network and retrieved depending on context.

This means, in practical terms, that these models can reuse different parts of their knowledge in a highly integrated way. Much like how your memory of a childhood vacation might resurface when triggered by a familiar smell or a snippet of a song, the neural network activates different pathways in response to different linguistic cues, allowing it to adapt quickly and flexibly to various kinds of inputs.

***

I have been engaging online occasionally with what I call the "Never AI" crowd, at least the more thoughtful ones. Partly that's to dispel misinformation, though I doubt I have much impact. Their opinions seem baked in. The bigger reason I make the attempt is to tease out how their thinking about AI and brains is different from mine.

I think I recently had a mini breakthrough in understanding some of the confusion, and distributed patterns are central it. I've had multiple people tell me, after several other dead-end reasons, that the reason AI can't be trusted is because all it does is analyze patterns.

To be clear, there are many reasons AI can't be trusted. But finding patterns isn't on the list.

Pattern analysis is the foundation of all intelligence—biological, artificial, and societal. From human cognition to market dynamics, intelligence emerges from identifying meaningful relationships in complex information. Brains, animals, AI, and whatever alien intelligence we might someday meet must have a way to interpret the world and take actions in it. There is no way to do that without finding patterns in the information the world presents. Even rule sets are pattern finders, albeit limited.

The notion that AI "just" analyzes patterns reveals a deeper misunderstanding about intelligence itself. Pattern recognition isn't a limitation: it's fundamental to how both natural and artificial intelligence work.

When I talk to many adults, it's clear they don't have the same understanding of patterns, or of networks, as I do. The "Never AI" and "it's optimal if every neuron fires" viewpoints are demonstrative of that.

Most schools teach about patterns and sometimes memory at early ages. It's an emphasis of Computational Thinking, for example, which describes a set of foundational, all-subject principles that are the bases for computer programming skills. AI requires the pattern and memory concepts be extended to statistical, large-scale, subtle, and distributed pattern types.

Complex networks and the properties they have infuse how I think about most large-scale issues. Many problems are inherently challenges over complex, associative networks, not unlike neural nets but usually with smarter "neurons," like entire people. Social networks, ecosystems, economies, bodies, and brains are all networked systems where the whole is greater than the sum of its parts.

AI remembers, but with a different paradigm than people are used to considering.

Today's version of rule-based systems are curated knowledge networks, usually called *knowledge graphs* but unrelated to data plots. You can think of this as a more sophisticated version of expert systems, where instead of the specification of rules there is the specification of relationships between aspects of knowledge. A biological knowledge graph might relate a disease state to symptoms, causes, medicines, prognoses, and whatever information is supported by evidence. These giant networks can then be mined based on various questions (e.g., what might be the cause of headache side effects after taking pain relievers?) that require connecting many different forms of knowledge. Knowledge graphs can be more flexibly applied than expert systems.

Some AI researchers believe it will take the fusion of data-driven (neural nets) and knowledge-driven (rules or knowledge network) approaches to advance AI to higher levels of cognition. They won't have to wait long, as that merger is beginning.

I still haven't gotten to the good stuff. What's AI doing when its neural network is cued by a pattern?

KEY META-PRINCIPLES

- **Patterns:** Patterns can capture nuance and complexity where rules fail.

- **Distributed memory:** Knowledge and memory exist across networks rather than isolated locations.

- **Collective emergence:** Complex behavior arises from the interaction of many simple elements.

- **Pattern cueing:** Memory and knowledge are stored contextually and retrieved based on related patterns.

EXAMPLE LEARNING PROGRESSION

K-5	• Identify and compare patterns in nature and everyday life. • Simulate group actions with simple rules to explore collective behaviors. • Create visual stories showing how systems work by recognizing patterns instead of strict rules.
6-8	• Analyze networks in nature or society to illustrate distributed memory. • Experiment with simple systems to show emergent behaviors. • Use examples like riddles or pattern puzzles to demonstrate pattern cueing over explicit instructions.
9-12	• Investigate distributed systems (e.g., ecosystems, markets) to analyze networked memory and collective emergence. • Create or simulate models showing patterns versus rules in real-world decision-making. • Explore how pattern cueing leads to context-specific decisions in AI and human systems.
College	• Study interdisciplinary systems (e.g., AI, social networks, economies) that exemplify distributed memory and emergence. • Design models or algorithms that prioritize patterns over rules for solving complex problems. • Critique the role of pattern cueing in intelligence, comparing its applications in AI and human cognition.

2.

TRANSFORMING

When people say, "AI recognizes patterns," they're actually describing three patterns dancing together. The first pattern is in the input data itself. The second pattern exists in the connections between artificial neurons—sometimes billions of weighted relationships that collectively form a complex filter. And the third pattern is what emerges on the other side.

Think of it as a stained-glass window. You have the pattern of light shining in (input), the pattern of colored glass pieces in the window (like the neural network's connection weights), and the pattern of colored light that falls on the inside wall (output). The window doesn't just block or allow light—it transforms everything based on its pattern of colored glass. The pattern on the inside wall is always some interaction between the incoming light and the window's design. The window's pattern actively changes every bit of light that passes through it, just as a neural network's pattern of connections *transforms* every piece of input data it processes.

A neural network doesn't simply match or reject input in a binary way. Instead, it transforms every input to some degree, with the transformation being stronger when the input pattern better aligns with what the network's connection pattern is tuned to detect. This is why AI can respond sensibly, if trained properly, even to inputs it has never seen before. There's always some degree of interaction between the patterns.

These transformations take several forms that should feel familiar. After all, teachers transform information all day long—

taking complex subjects and making them grade-appropriate, turning abstract concepts into concrete examples, and translating student behavior into meaningful feedback. AI's transformations aren't so different. Whether you're teaching fractions using pizza slices or having AI turn text into speech, you're engaging in the art of information transformation.

There are also a few ways neural networks—or any intelligent system—transform information that are like the Ginsu knife commercials I saw as a kid ("It can dice, slice, even julienne fries!"). They're extremely important to lots of applications.

The most important transformations are *categorizations* and *regressions* that transform data to what's usually a small number of outputs that provide some kind of generalized insight. But there are also important applications where the number of output information channels after transformation is large too, just like the input. No matter what the transformation, a pattern at the input interacts with a pattern in the network connection strengths to produce an output pattern.

I'll describe the main ways AI transforms information because they are the ways people morph information too. And just like that stained-glass window, understanding these transformations helps us see things in a whole new light.

The general notion of transformation is of course taught in school in other guises, whether through studying butterflies and moths, government and political shifts, or character evolution in literature. But pattern transformations aren't typical teaching points.

The key information isn't that the transformation happens, but that certain kinds of transformations are so fundamental that they practically structure how any intelligence must parse the world.

Much of AI's progress comes not just from bigger or faster systems, but from creative insights about what kinds of transformations are possible and useful. The shift from narrow AI applications (like spam detection or image recognition) to general-purpose GenAI exemplifies this kind of creative leap. Engineers theorized that many seemingly different tasks could be recast into a single type of pattern recognition problem. For AI language models, that task is deciding the next characters to output. Those choices are categorizations, one of the most common AI transformations.

Sometimes AI use requires specialized pattern transformations. For example, Google researchers realized dance movements could be represented as patterns that relate to musical patterns. That transformation opened new possibilities in computer choreography.[47] Meta's AudioGen tranforms sound waves into visual scenes.[48] Researchers have shown how neural signals from the brain's speech areas can be transformed directly into synthesized speech.[49] Signals from the brain's neural net pass through an AI's neural net to figure out what speech the brain signals represent.

Neural networks can learn incredibly diverse types of transformations. DeepMind's work on context learning shows how AI can transform observations of varying situations into adaptive behaviors.[50] This demonstrates that a neural net's transformation power is not limited by the abstraction level of the pattern.

I'll describe AI's most common information transformations.

PREPROCESSING

There is a certain amount of transformation needed before the neural network gets to do anything with the input data. That's called *preprocessing*, and it decides how to represent information and its context to a neural net. It's like lesson preparation.

Whether in support of an AI or a human judgment, the way content is represented can have a dramatic effect on how it's understood and acted upon.

Representations affect people for sure. Presenting numbers in a table offers a different perception than showing the same data in a graph. A graph might highlight trends and patterns that aren't immediately obvious in a table of numbers. How we represent information shapes our interpretation.

In human psychology, framing can have an enormous effect.[51] A doctor might tell a patient that a surgery has a "90% survival rate," which sounds reassuring. Alternatively, saying there's a "10% mortality rate" conveys the same statistics but feels more alarming. The way information is represented could change the patient's decision making.

AI is also sensitive to representation. Giving it a table of numbers activates the neural net differently than a plot image that is based on the table. It's hard to say whether AI will be affected in a similar way as people by the representation choice, but the interpretation will differ somehow.

Some information is typically represented in ways neural nets don't like. They like numbers. Just numbers. Not characters that represent numbers, but numbers that math runs on.

Before AI can process text or other non-numeric data, engineers must first convert the information into numbers. Typical software can handle text directly because coding languages understand text as a special form of data. AI neural networks, however, are pure math beasts. They take in numbers, calculate across all the neurons, and output numbers.

There are various forms of data that must be converted to numbers, including text and language, images, categorical information like labels or ratings, and temporal data about time and sequences. Somehow that information has got to morph into numbers. The key is doing so in a way that maintains the information's essential relationships.

Images, for example, are just numbers. But those numbers can represent different intensity and color-coding schemes. AI also needs to know that there is a spatial relationship between the pixels, though that's handled more explicitly by making the neural network two-dimensional and including neurons that focus on a region of the image.

Categorical data like colors, sizes, or ratings present a special challenge when converting to numbers. You can't simply assign numbers like 1, 2, 3 to categories like "red", "blue", and "green" because that would falsely suggest that blue is somehow between red and green. Instead, AI systems use methods that give each category its own separate numerical flag or create a mathematical construct where similar categories are grouped together. The key is preserving which categories are distinct from each other while also maintaining any natural relationships, like how "freezing" and "cold" are more similar to each other than either is to "hot."

Text requires careful conversion to numbers to preserve both meaning and structure, a process called *embedding*. Some pretty sophisticated math is used. In the end, words are made into a list of numbers, not a single number. Text is turned into a numerical pattern. Improved embedding methods have been critical in AI language model advancement.[52]

The embedding transformation makes similar words like "cat" and "kitten" have similar number patterns. The transformation also needs to track word order, since meaning often depends on arrangement. Though the math is not important to the typical student, language embeddings can be used to visualize similarity between words that could be useful in relaying language nuances.

Sometimes the innovation is the information representation. Physicists at CERN developed new ways to use AI to identify particle collision patterns.[53] Rather than trying to analyze detector data directly, they transformed the problem into one of analyzing the relationships between particles. By innovating the input data representation, CERN scientists got significant improvements in particle detection and classification.

CONTEXT IS THE NEW METADATA

Beyond the raw data itself, there's a crucial layer of information that shapes how AI systems understand and process their inputs.

It has traditionally been called metadata, which means data about data—when it was created, who created it, what format it's in, and so on. If it's a photo, metadata could be notes about when and where it was taken, who's in it, and what was happening at the time. Metadata is context that helps organize and properly interpret the information.

GenAI expands the concept of metadata and democratizes the responsibility. Information representation is also an AI user's responsibility, not just an AI engineer one.

Luckily, information representation for our use of AI doesn't require complex math. Rather, it's about how we describe the context to the AI for its task and choose knowledge to upload.

Contextual information shapes how the AI processes and responds to requests. This includes factors like tone, style preferences, intended audience, purpose, cultural context, level of formality, technical depth, and ethical considerations. A teacher would give different explanations of the same concept to a first grader versus a high school student, and so will AI. An article would be written differently for a technical journal versus a general audience newspaper. AI would think so too.

Our view of context is incredibly important when working with AI systems. GenAI is stuck in its text (and now audio, image, and video) world. They need explicit guidance about contextual factors to provide appropriate responses. It's like the difference between asking someone for directions in person, where they can see if you're walking or driving and adjust accordingly, versus writing directions that need to explicitly state all assumptions and conditions.

Context for AI is different than context for people in two giant regards.

One is that AI is not sharing the rest of your life and world at the time you use it. It isn't informed about aspects of the task environment that another person would easily notice. AI can't know anything about you and your task environment unless it is provided the information. Without explicit context, AI defaults to generic assumptions and responses. The AI operates like a transfer student who just walked into class five minutes before the bell, and has no idea who the teacher is, what's on the test, or why everyone's giggling at an inside joke it never heard.

A second difference is people often share tacit information. If two educators in your school are asked to create a lesson plan for a specific learning objective, they will probably be more similar than two teachers from different schools. There are aspects of structure (e.g., class times), student population, pedagogy, and expectations that cultures will share, often in unspoken ways.

Directing AI's output representations is also critically important. The skills of information representation and context have value here too. The same underlying data can tell vastly different stories depending on how it's presented.

Students need to understand these principles not just for working with AI, but for effective communication in general. When they recognize how different representations affect understanding, they become better at choosing how to present their own work and critically evaluate information they receive. They learn to consider their audience and purpose when deciding how to represent information, with the special case of especially context-needy AI.

Representation and context are like setting the right oven temperature for a recipe to succeed, but your recipe still must have a purpose. The AI transformation needs a purpose.

The usual AI purposes are common task types that aren't going to go away, ever, because they are necessary for any intelligence to structure information.

MAKING SENSE OF INFORMATION

Imagine you're a data scientist at a dating app company called "HeartBytes" Your job is to understand what makes matches successful.

You've plotted data from lots of couples, as shown in Figure 3. Each point represents a potential dating app match, labeled according to whether the pairing was eventually "successful" or "unsuccessful." The horizontal axis shows how many interests they share (scaled 0-100), while the vertical axis shows how many hours they chatted before meeting in person. The scatter plot is a mess of points that looks like someone sprinkled confetti across your screen. But in that apparent chaos often lies patterns.

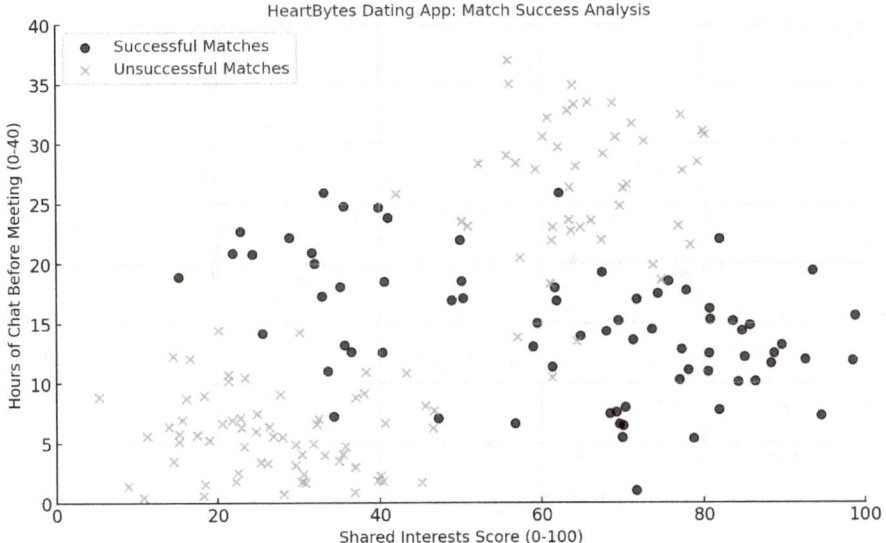

Figure 3. Hypothetical distribution of HeartBytes data. The data set and plot were generated by ChatGPT-4o in December 2024.

This messy data reflects a challenge that any intelligence faces, whether neurons or silicon. How do you extract meaning from raw information? It turns out there are several fundamental ways to structure information, and at an abstract level both brains and AI use remarkably similar approaches.

There are different lenses for viewing the same reality. Just as you might look at a mountain range through regular binoculars, infrared goggles, or a geological survey map, each revealing different aspects of the same landscape, there are multiple ways to analyze information.

I'll describe four fundamental ways intelligence can derive meaning from information. Think of these four operations as the AI's version of sorting laundry, guessing your shirt size, deciding which shirt to wear first, and maybe turning your T-shirt into a pillowcase. Each transformation makes sense of the information chaos in different ways.

I'll use the imaginary dating app as an example.

First, we might want to categorize—drawing boundaries that separate "successful match" from "unsuccessful match" regions. Looking at the scatter plot in Figure 3, you might notice that couples with both high shared interests and moderate chat times tend to be successful (black dots). We could draw a boundary around this "sweet spot," creating categories of promising and unpromising matches.

But what if we want more nuance than just "successful" or "unsuccessful"? That's where regression comes in. Instead of drawing hard boundaries, AI could fit a curve that predicts the probability of a successful match based on our variables. This gives us a continuous measure, like saying there's a 75% chance of success rather than a simple yes/no prediction.

Sometimes what matters isn't the absolute likelihood of success but how potential matches compare to each other. This is where *ranking* comes in. Given limited time, our dating app users might want to know which potential matches they should prioritize, regardless of the exact odds of success.

Finally, we might want to transform these patterns into entirely different representations. We might convert our match likelihood patterns into recommended chat lengths for different interest levels, or into guidelines for when to suggest meeting in person.

These four operations—categorization, regression, ranking, and representation transformation—are fundamental ways that any intelligence, artificial or biological, must structure information to make sense of the world. When you recognize a friend's face (categorization), estimate how long a task will take (regression), decide which task to do first (ranking), or translate a concept from one language to another (representation transformation), you're using these same basic operations.

CATEGORIZATION

Looking at the HeartBytes data, the simplest question we might ask is: "Will this match work out?" It's a yes-or-no categorization that tries to divide the data examples into two clear groups. (Technically, it's a classification, which is a categorization into non-overlapping buckets.)

But where exactly do we draw the boundary of the "successful" category?

We can mentally draw a boundary around the dark data points. The matches that didn't work either had many shared interests but chatted too much before meeting, or didn't have many shared interests and didn't chat long enough.

I have hand-drawn (not calculated) potential boundaries between successful and unsuccessful matches, as shown in Figure 4.

There are a few key observations to make about categorization boundaries. First, misclassifications are inevitable for most real-world problems. No matter where the boundary is drawn, some matches will end up on the wrong side. In the HeartBytes example, certain couples who were ultimately successful might fall outside the defined "success" zone, while some that didn't work out could be mistakenly included. Real-world information is rarely neatly separable.

Second, there isn't a single "correct" way to draw the boundary for this example. The successful matches in the scatter plot might be enclosed by a curved shape that wraps around them tightly, or simpler boundaries like the ones drawn. Both choices have trade-offs. A complex, flexible boundary might fit the data better but could overcomplicate the model, making it too sensitive to minor variations. A simpler boundary, on the other hand, might be easier to interpret but less precise. The right decision depends on the goal—whether the priority is precision, simplicity, or generalizability.

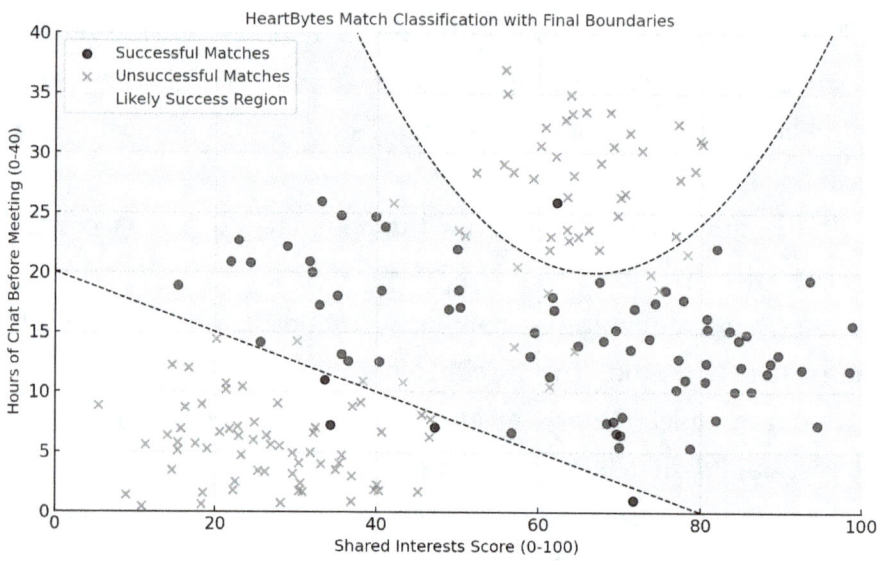

Figure 4. Hypothetical categorization boundaries that divide successful and unsuccessful matches. The data set and plot were generated by ChatGPT-4o in December 2024.

A third, related challenge is dealing with unknown regions. There are areas of the scatter plot where there are no data points at all. If an AI model is asked to categorize a match in one of these blank spaces, it has no direct experience to rely on. It will still provide an answer, but that answer will be more uncertain than those based on well-represented regions of the dataset. This is one of the fundamental difficulties in categorization: whenever we divide things into groups, we inevitably create gray areas where the right classification is ambiguous.

Defining the right categories requires a balance between clarity and flexibility, and understanding these limitations helps us use AI's categorization abilities more effectively. Intelligence—whether natural or artificial—must grapple with this uncertainty. One approach is to use probabilistic categories: instead of a hard yes/no boundary, we might say a match falls "80% in the success category." Another approach is to use multiple overlapping categories: a match might be categorized as both "high compatibility" and "needs more chat time."

Modern AI systems work with far more than two features. They might consider thousands or millions of characteristics simultaneously. While we can't visualize this imaginary high-dimensional space, the principles remain the same. The categorizing AI creates boundaries in an umpteen-dimensional scatter plot, dividing it into regions corresponding to different categories.

AI's ability to handle so much information also means the AI developer doesn't need to make feature choices. For example, the "Shared Interest Score" (the x-axis), is something the HeartBytes analyst must have come up with. It's some measure that uses user profile information, but in an unclear way. Maybe the categories would be more cleanly separable with a different measure. Since AI can chew on a lot, those subjective choices aren't in play anymore. An AI developer would just give the AI all of the user data and have it find the cleanest separation in that giant, imaginary scatter plot.

The categories we choose depend on our goals. The HeartBytes data analyst divided matches into success/failure categories because they wanted to steer interactions toward more productive outcomes. For the business, a productive outcome might be if users feel their money was well spent, and that probably depends upon them getting a match they see as promising. Yet there are other ways of slicing the information according to different goals. Perhaps it would be better for the business if people didn't match too well and leave the service but rather have a series of short-term relationships that keep them on the platform. That's where a lot of our troubles begin. A company's goal is not necessarily our goal, nor society's. In any event, it would mean categorizing using a different outcome measurement.

Good category choices should be distinct enough to be meaningful, similar enough within categories to be useful groupings, different enough that the categorization enables action, and aligned with the goals of humans. There's tremendous creativity just in deciding how to group information.

When you interact with AI, you're often implicitly telling it which categories matter for your current task. Even something as seemingly simple as "Act like a teacher" is a directive to AI to categorize information into "like teacher" or not, and only output "like teacher" stuff. And just as different cultures might categorize colors or emotions differently, AI systems can develop different categorization schemes depending on their training and objectives.

For example, I had a discussion in 2023 with ChatGPT-4 about what it considers the difference between a teacher and an instructional designer in the context of educational game design. It basically said a teacher will have a focus on instruction that might mitigate the value of the game experience, spending more time on imparting information. It said the teacher might cave and provide too many hints. ChatGPT said the instructional designer was more likely to allow the experience to teach, and balance hints and challenge better.

That's probably not true, but high skill use of AI means we understand the implication of our categorization choices as AI sees it. Only then can we attempt to morph its perspective appropriately.

Categorization isn't just about organizing things; it's about creating meaning. When we decide what categories matter and how to define them, we're making decisions about what distinctions are important. There is a fundamental tension between simplification and accuracy that all categorizations face. Group people according to the wrong criteria and it might stereotype. But usually, you have to pick some way of dividing up the world, even if it needs gray boundaries or an "uncertain" category.

Meta-knowledge about categorization is super useful. For example, when you ask AI to make a categorization judgment like deciding whether a particular paragraph can be written better, then you might want to define the threshold for changing something, even vaguely. There must be a "change" or "don't change" boundary, and you want the AI to judge the boundary similarly. Your description of what is considered for the editorial classification tells the AI what features are most relevant to the judgment. Choose wisely.

Boundary Cases

When examples are provided to train AI on a categorization decision, we need to provide the most impactful ones. If we only show the AI typical cases, it won't learn where the boundaries of the categories should be. We need examples near the edges of categories to define them properly. Example student assignments that are barely above or below the 'B'-plus / 'A'-minus boundary will help the AI make subtle grading decisions better than solid 'A' and 'B' exemplars.

The concept of boundary cases is powerful across disciplines. In science, boundary cases help define the limits of theories. In writing, they help students understand genre conventions and word choice. In ethics, they help explore moral principles. AI can help generate these boundary cases, creating examples that challenge our category definitions. It's also useful to probe AI's understanding of the boundary by asking it to generate a boundary example.

One basic thing you learn developing AI to make decisions is that you need to give training examples on each side of the category boundary. That's not only true for AI; it's true for decisions in general.

Think about that for your classroom, because AI can unlock new possibilities. For example, a key literacy skill is recognizing skilled writing. After all, people need to intuit when their own writing needs improvement. Teachers likely have students read from a bunch of skilled writers. Do they compare those works with a similar story from a less skilled writer? Can they recognize the steps on the way to greatness? Students need to see good work and bad work to be able to fully tell the difference. Who has time to write those variants? I'd trust AI with that one, especially since perfection isn't the goal!

Understanding categorization also helps in recognizing ill-posed tasks. When AI makes surprising categorization errors, it's often because the chosen features don't capture important distinctions, or the category boundaries are genuinely ambiguous. Students might struggle with their own categorization tasks for similar reasons, because of limited exposure to examples, attention to irrelevant features, or confusion about category boundaries.

AI Detection

When categorizing anything there's an unavoidable trade-off. For the dating app, moving the boundary for successful matches changes which borderline cases fall into each category, but there's no free lunch. If more successful matches are included, then some unsuccessful matches will come along. If the boundary is made tighter to avoid these false positives, then some genuinely good matches will be excluded. This trade-off is illustrated by the notional Receiver Operating Characteristic (ROC) curve in Figure 5.

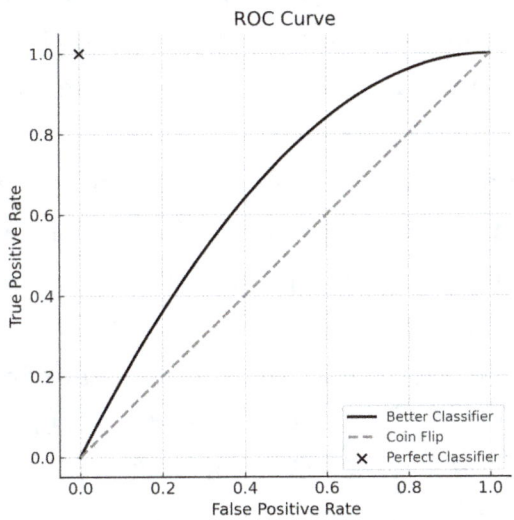

Figure 5. A notional ROC curve illustration, generated by ChatGPT-4o on February 12, 2025.

Each point on the curve represents a different classification threshold. Moving up the curve increases true positives but also raises false positives. Moving down reduces false positives but excludes more true positives. A curve that bows toward the upper left corner indicates clearer separation than one closer to the diagonal line. Each point on the ROC curve is a valid operating point for the classifier. Which point is chosen is dependent on operational tolerances for missed detections or false alarms.

Tools that tell you they're detecting AI writing are binary classifiers, but their ROC curve is relatively flat, explaining why the performance of AI detectors struggle. Their task is like trying to draw a boundary between two overlapping clouds of points, where AI-written and human-written text share many characteristics. To catch most AI writing, they must draw a wide boundary that inevitably includes some human writing. To avoid falsely accusing students of cheating, they must draw a tight boundary that misses much AI content. There's no perfect boundary—just different balances of these competing errors.

The trade-off gets harder as AI writing becomes more sophisticated and varied. The "clouds" of AI-written and human-written text increasingly overlap, making any boundary less effective at separating them.

As an educator, you are likely better at identifying AI-generated writing than detectors because you understand your students' history and context—something AI lacks. You don't need a technical crutch. Even with that advantage, you are more likely to catch students who misuse AI rather than those who use it skillfully, and you will sometimes be wrong.[54]

REGRESSION

While categorizing HeartBytes matches into "successful" or "unsuccessful" might be useful, it misses a lot of nuances. Real relationships aren't binary. They exist on a spectrum from disaster to soulmates with plenty of territory in between.

This is where regression comes in. Instead of drawing boundaries between categories, regression fits a continuous curve through the data, in this case trying to predict exactly how successful a match might be.

Many educators will recognize regression from their encounters with curve fitting in math classes. When students plot points on a graph and draw a line of best fit, they're performing the simplest kind of regression—linear regression. The line represents a rule that predicts y-values from x-values, trying to get as close as possible to all the data points.

Regression isn't limited to straight lines. AI can learn much more complex relationships between inputs and outputs. The principle remains the same. AI must find a rule (whether a simple line or a complex curve) that best predicts the desired values. The main difference is scale and complexity. While students might fit a line to a dozen points with two variables, AI systems can fit complex patterns to millions of points with thousands of variables.

Regression tasks appear everywhere in life, and in AI applications. When AI predicts house prices or product sales, it's performing regression. When your travel app estimates how long a trip will take based on traffic and weather, it's performing a kind of regression.

Instead of sorting items into buckets, regression is trying to pinpoint specific values. Regression and categorization are kind of opposite one another. Whereas categorization defines distinctions between information, regression defines relationships.

Regression might seem more precise than categorization, but it comes with its own challenges. The categorization challenge is finding the boundary; in regression it's the metric. All the input information is being squeezed down into one number. The way that metric is defined is critical. A movie recommendation AI needs to do regression over a "likelihood to want to watch" score that consists of many factors. If that score weights my one-off viewing history too heavily, maybe I'll be served an endless lineup of slow, subtitled art-house films just because I fell asleep during one obscure documentary.

If each point in the HeartBytes scatter plot were given a match likelihood score instead of just a category, then regression could try to find a meandering curve that keeps increasing from lowest to highest match likelihood. The curve would be a statistical fit, as with linear regression. The match likelihood score is independent of the density of the data points in the scatter plot. That density is more dependent on the prevalence of the couple combinations.

The ability to map complex relationships is why regression is fundamental to both human and artificial intelligence.

RANKING

Sometimes the exact score doesn't matter as much as how options compare to each other. If you're using HeartBytes and have limited time, you might care less about whether a potential match scores 75 or 85, and more about which of your current matches you should prioritize.

Ranking transforms absolute measures into relative positions. Instead of saying Match A scores 75 and Match B scores 85, ranking simply says B is better than A. This might seem like a loss of information compared to regression—and it is—but it's often exactly what we need. Many real-world decisions don't require knowing precise values, just which option to choose first. Think search engine results.

Ranking can capture patterns that both categorization and regression might miss. It forces us to decide a relative priority, which often aligns better with how we actually make decisions. This is why ranking is its own fundamental operation, distinct from categorization or regression. It's about ordering rather than grouping or measuring.

Ranking sits at an interesting intersection between categorization and regression. We can think of ranking as imposing discrete categories (1st, 2nd, 3rd, etc.) onto what's often an underlying continuous scale (like test scores, relevance scores, or performance metrics). In this sense, ranking is a categorization of a regression.

In practice, people or AI don't have to decide on the rating scale, as they would with regression. They can rank through a series of pairwise comparisons, à la what Mark Zuckerberg was doing with his initial Facebook software (however odious).[55] When Netflix suggests shows you might like, it's not trying to predict exact ratings, but rather which shows should appear first in your feed. When your brain decides which task to tackle next, it's performing a ranking operation on your to-do list.

Ranking also reveals a key principle about intelligence. Sometimes less precision enables better decisions. By focusing on relative position rather than absolute values, ranking can be more robust to noise and uncertainty in the data. It's often easier (and more useful) to know that Option A is better than Option B than to precisely quantify how much better it is. Humans are also generally more mentally sensitive to relative differences (ranking) than to absolute ones (regression).[56]

The accuracy of regression and ranking often depends on having enough examples across the full range of possibilities. Just as categorization needs examples near category boundaries, regression needs examples across the full scale of possible values, and ranking needs examples at various levels of the hierarchy.

Understanding these approaches helps us use AI more effectively. When we ask AI to critique writing, for instance, we might want categorization ("Is this appropriate for a business email?"), regression ("What grade level is this written at?"), or ranking ("Which of these drafts is best?"). Being clear about which type of judgment we want helps us both frame our requests better (e.g. what examples to offer) and interpret AI's responses more accurately.

REPRESENTATION TRANSFORMATION

Sometimes we don't need to decide with data, but we just want to put it into another form that's more suitable for some situation. This is representation transformation—changing the form of information while trying to preserve its essential meaning. I talked about changing representations in the context of preprocessing, but it can also be the primary function of the AI.

Data compression is a representation transformation that tries to preserve meaning but reduce storage space. Some compression techniques are "lossy," meaning they knowingly give up some information, but the art is in giving away as little information meaning as possible while decreasing storage size.

Our brains seamlessly transform between different sensory representations, converting the visual pattern of written words into their sonic equivalents or translating abstract concepts into concrete examples. When you read "sweet," your brain might activate taste sensations, memories of desserts, or emotional associations. Representation transformation is a necessary part of such associations.

AI performs similar transformations constantly. When AI turns text into images, it's transforming between representational formats. When it converts speech to text, or summarizes a long document into key points, it's preserving meaning while changing form, albeit in a lossy way. Even language translation is fundamentally about maintaining meaning across different representational systems.

While categorization divides, regression measures, and ranking orders, representation transformation preserves patterns while changing their format. It's not extracting new meaning but is expressing existing meaning in new ways.

The quality of representation transformation often depends on how well the new format captures important patterns from the original. For example, AI-generated images are only meaningful if they capture the essence of the text prompts that inspired them.

Our brains have dedicated significant neural real estate to representation transformation. The parietal lobe, and especially a region called the angular gyrus, specializes in converting information between different forms.[57] This area helps us transform written words into their sounds, connect numbers to their quantities, and integrate information from different senses into coherent experiences.[58] When you see the number "7" and automatically sense its "seven-ness," or read the word "rough" and feel its texture in your mind, your angular gyrus is performing representation transformation. That our brains evolved specific machinery for this operation hints at just how fundamental it is to intelligence.

Together, these four fundamental operations—categorization, regression, ranking, and representation transformation—form the basic toolkit that any intelligence uses to make sense of patterns. Whether you're analyzing dating matches or teaching AI, understanding these operations helps reveal how intelligence structures and reframes information.

***

In 2022 I did a bit of consultation for biotech and pharmaceutical companies, mostly about how AI might help drug discovery and the clinical trial process. This kind of analysis certainly includes technology assessment, but the human and organizational aspects matter just as much. The question I was trying to answer for these companies wasn't just whether a technology could do something and how hard that might be, but whether it would matter given the human decisions and influences in the company.

I asked a simple question early in the process to get at the decisions that are the most important drivers of the business. Often it was something like "how do you decide which of the drugs you're exploring should get additional investment, and which should be dropped?" Each drug candidate needs ratings (regressions) against various squishy criteria that relate in some way to safety and efficacy. And ultimately, they need to be ranked and budgeted.

I usually couldn't pin down how they made the decisions. The choices are incremental, with company politics and power centers a major factor. Other times, it's clear a single person made the most important choices the company can make entirely on their own, using logic others are not told. Often, it's the CEO, and sometimes that person is far less informed than others in the organization.

People believe their decisions are unbiased and informed. But usually, they could have been more thoroughly considered, especially by using decision processes that try to mitigate our psychological weaknesses.

Not all decisions warrant deep scrutiny, but major ones demand a structured process. A key part of collective decisions is coming to a common understanding of categories, ratings (regression), ranking, and representations. People try to agree on definitions, but for complex decisions this is often not helpful. It'd be like trying to write a definition for intelligence to tell you what AI can do. We could all read the same definition, and if by some miracle we agree on it, I bet we still would categorize "intelligent" and "not intelligent" differently for specific examples.

For something like drug discovery, the effect of decisions can't be known for a long time. The same is true for education. There's not enough feedback to become a better decision maker quickly, which is why it can take decades of experience to build certain judgment skills.

The way to learn how a person or organization makes decisions is by giving them a bunch of decisions and analyzing the classification boundary, the rank order, or some other aspects of the decision. It's one way to find out if the people in the company are on the same page, and to use the differences in choices as fodder for innovation or improvement.

Humanity has been making hand-wavy decisions for a long time. As Daniel Kahneman, lead guru in the realm of judgment psychology, said "I'm very impressed, actually, by the combination of curiosity and resistance that I encounter. The thing that astonishes me when I talk to businesspeople in the context of decision analysis is that you have an organization that's making lots of decisions and they're not keeping track. They're not trying to learn from their own mistakes; they're not investing the smallest amount in trying to actually figure out what they've done wrong. And that's not an accident: They don't want to know."

There has been very little corporate or societal effort to make better decisions. People do not like to give up decision power, and almost everyone thinks they make better decisions than others. But we know from many studies that human decisions have a ton of flaws.

I have not seen research on whether AI inherits some human psychological biases, but if it justifies decisions more clearly, will it take on greater decision-making roles? If it becomes clearer that we stink at making important decisions, then AI will make more of them.

People need more structured decision processes in the era of AI, at least for high-impact decisions. That often involves debates over information transformations. Students need a lot of decision practice to understand how they, others, and AI are judging.

KEY META-PRINCIPLES

- **Information Representation**: The structure and format of data affect how it is processed and interpreted.

- **Context Shapes Understanding**: Context influences how information is transformed, whether by humans or AI.

- **Types of Transformations**: The four main types of transformations—categorization, regression, ranking, and representation transformation—are foundational for how AI (and humans) process and act on information.

- **Prompting for Transformation**: Understanding how prompts affect transformations allows users to guide GenAI effectively.

EXAMPLE LEARNING PROGRESSION

K-5	• Explore how changing the format of information highlights different aspects of the same data. • Play games to sort and categorize objects, words, or pictures into groups based on simple features. • Practice asking clear questions or giving examples to guide others in completing tasks.
6-8	• Analyze how context changes meaning by providing or interpreting examples. • Identify the types of transformations in tasks or real-life scenarios. • Write clear instructions or prompts for peers to achieve specific transformations.
9-12	• Experiment with how representation choices affect interpretation and decision-making. • Apply transformation types to real-world scenarios conceptually and through GenAI tools. • Develop and refine prompts or examples to guide AI outputs, focusing on clarity and relevance to desired transformations.
College	• Evaluate the implications of representation and context in AI transformations. • Design and execute tasks that demonstrate mastery of transformation types. • Critically assess the relationship between prompting strategies, transformations, and outcomes in GenAI applications.

3.

KNOWING

AI developers create software that performs complex tasks beyond conventional programming, often rivaling human abilities. You might think there are lively debates in AI engineering offices worldwide about what it means for the machine to "think," "know," "understand," or be "intelligent."

That wasn't my experience—it seemed more common among AI newcomers. Those who have been around AI long enough have tussled with those questions early on if they were philosophically inclined.

But after the ChatGPT cannonball, the philosophers have emerged. And they are ticked. Much of the emotion is tied to the specialness of humans that is baked into our psyche. In that sense, the ChatGPT moment was Copernican or Darwinian.

Many of them dislike assigning humanistic terms to what is, at heart, computer software. They don't like anthropomorphizing. The irked say AI can't know or understand, and it's certainly not intelligent. And if someone says AI consciousness or sentience, then you'd better stand back.

The meaning of terms like think, know, understand, or intelligent have been stretched by the evolution of philosophy, the invention of computers, and studies of other animals. Some are uncomfortable with those shifts.

At a practical level, these philosophical debates are unproductive rabbit holes. They just don't affect decisions about AI.

There are other reasons to bring it up. These debates influence how we perceive AI and the level of respect we afford it. Opponents of anthropomorphism are usually trying to downplay AI and idealize humans—both misleading perspectives. And honestly, in the future we may be debating moral questions about advanced AI and how we treat it that rely upon philosophical principles.

You may have noticed that I usually ditch the quotes when AI is attributed a cognitive term. It gets tiresome, and I often don't have other terms to use that won't be considered strictly human as well.

Does AI remember? Surely. I've already covered that.

Does it know? I feel confident saying yes.

Understand? I'm not sure.

Sentient? No.

But the story is more nuanced.

KNOWLEDGE, UNDERSTANDING, AND SENTIENCE

The nature, origin, and scope of knowledge, specifically human knowledge, is the subject of the philosophical domain called epistemology.

AI clearly remembers, but going from memory to knowledge requires attributes AI lacks, according to classical epistemology. The biggest ones are belief and consciousness.

Classical philosophy about knowledge goes back at least as far as Plato, who defined it as "justified true belief."[59] It means one believes something, the belief is true, and one has justification for the belief.

This seems to be where people get upset. Subjects in school are often taught as history lessons, placing undue emphasis on the past. Biology classes can spend more time on Gregor Mendel's pea pods than modern genetics, and philosophy classes love the classical philosophers. My guess is the anthropomorphism outrage stems from a Platonic view that knowledge requires deliberation (to have belief and justification), and seemingly the need for consciousness.

Over the past several decades, philosophers and scientists have dramatically changed how we think about knowledge.

For example, being right for the wrong reasons isn't really knowledge, even if you can justify it, like correctly guessing tomorrow's weather based on a broken thermometer.[60]

Philosophers also see knowledge in reliable processes and social interactions in addition to individual reasoning.[61] Think of how scientific knowledge develops.[62] Community interaction generates knowledge that's different from, and often richer than, purely individual learning. Power dynamics matter too. Who gets heard and whose ideas are taken seriously shapes what becomes accepted as knowledge.[63]

These insights have pushed philosophers to look at how knowledge develops in human minds and communities, rather than just thinking about it abstractly.[64] Knowledge is now understood as something that emerges from the complex ways people interact with each other and their environment.

Neuroscience and psychology are influences too. As far as scientists can tell, everything our nervous systems know and understand—even consciousness itself—can be turned off by adjusting one or more part of the brain. Plato didn't consider the possibility that any part of the body is significantly involved in true cognition. He believed knowledge came from recalling truths from an all-knowing soul that existed before entering our physical form.

Plato overlooked unconscious knowledge. When a teacher can tell a student is about to act out before obvious signs appear, is that "justified true belief"? Where was the deliberation? The skill is unconscious, built through years of experience.

Nobel laureate Daniel Kahneman clarifies this kind of knowing in *Thinking, Fast and Slow*.[65] He describes two systems in our brain. System 2 is our conscious mind—slow, deliberative, and frankly rather lazy. System 1, our unconscious mind, is where most of the action happens. It's fast, intuitive, and constantly analyzing patterns. That teacher's knowledge of impending classroom disruption is System 1 at work.

While there are similarities between our unconscious processing and AI's pattern analysis, two significant distinctions stand out. First, our unconscious isn't very verbal. It deals in impressions, feelings, and intuitions that our conscious mind later tries to explain but fundamentally wasn't let in on. AI language models, on the other hand, are inherently verbal since text is their reality. Second, these language models learn from our conscious writings, not (yet) from world experience, though that's a giant focus of AI research. They're pattern-matching on what humans deliberately wrote down or imaged or recorded, not learning directly from experiencing the world like we do.

AI language models are a System 1 type of processing on our System 2 output. It looks for patterns in our conscious thinking. That can make AI appear to reason when it's really pattern analyzing on our reasoning. (I'm not yet considering iterative "reasoning" that many GenAI models now use, which is addressed in Volume 2.)

If our unconscious "knows" and that doesn't require explicit belief or justification, then AI "knows" too. So does a dog.

Understanding, however, is supposedly deeper than mere knowledge.

Aristotle viewed understanding (epistêmê) as a purely rational grasp of universal principles and their causes, requiring conscious deliberation and explicit reasoning.[66] Medieval philosophers following this tradition emphasized that real understanding required the ability to explain.[67] The view was you don't truly understand something unless you can articulate why it was true and how it connects to other truths.

Fast forward to the mid-20th century, and now we're in the sweet spot for educators. Bloom's Taxonomy placed understanding as a crucial step between basic recall and higher-order thinking, suggesting a hierarchy of cognitive processes.[68] Jerome Bruner expanded this view, arguing that understanding means grasping the structure of a subject, the key ideas and relationships that make everything hang together.[69] These frameworks still shape how we think about teaching and learning today.

But again, views have evolved, and the new perspectives might not have penetrated education.

The social and collaborative nature of some forms of understanding has been made clear, as with knowledge.[70]

Cognitive scientists and neuroscientists have shown that much of understanding, not just knowledge, exists in our unconscious.[71,72] There are even various levels of consciousness.[73] When a jazz musician improvises or a chef creates a new dish, they're drawing on deep wells of implicit knowledge that they might never be able to fully articulate. This kind of understanding is encoded in the very patterns of our neural networks, shaped by experience and practice.

Is understanding encoded in AI's neural network? When a large language model makes connections between different topics or applies knowledge in novel ways, is that understanding?

If you think understanding requires its own beliefs and intentions, particularly the ability to generate its own, then no, AI doesn't understand. (With the emergence of AI agents, this barrier will begin dissolving. Agents are also discussed in Volume 2.)

But that's the old, classical view. If understanding is about associating knowledge and applying it to novel problems, then AI does that too, although inconsistently.

The elephant in the room is consciousness. Belief and intentionality that are seen in classical philosophies as critical to knowing and understanding rely on consciousness. As I've indicated, much "knowing" and "understanding" is done in the unconscious or through collective interactions, but clearly conscious deliberation is needed for much of "understanding." I think it's on that plank that most anthropomorphism objections ride.

For many reasons, few believe AI is sentient. Though we can't definitively know one way or the other, it doesn't appear current AI is all that close to the boundary line.

I happen to think consciousness isn't that important in terms of AI abilities. AI could get superhuman without it. Think how well it's doing against humans already on many types of tasks.

I don't claim to be a philosophy expert, and debating deeply philosophical issues can quickly become dizzying. But I think what can come across as principled definitions and rationales are usually predicated on putting human beings on a pedestal.

Knowledge and understanding come in more varieties than we've traditionally recognized. And AI sentience isn't necessary for super-human skill.

Does AI remember? Yep, no doubt.

Does it know? As with our subconscious, it's hard to argue against AI knowing too.

Understand? I think sometimes.

Is it sentient? No. On that there's little disagreement.

Could it be? If you think all human abilities and qualities are generated within our bodies, then yes AI could eventually be able to mimic all brain functions, including consciousness, though it might require biological processing. Mimicking the brain is probably not the only way to get there, and we don't know on which of the other paths consciousness might emerge, or if it's inevitable beyond some intelligence level.

Will we be able to tell when and if AI becomes conscious? No. At a practical level, I cannot know that anyone but myself is conscious, and they cannot prove it to me. Subjective experience in other beings cannot be proven or disproven. This is known as the "problem of other minds" in consciousness research.[74]

It may not ultimately matter whether we can definitively prove that an AI is conscious. If it exhibits behaviors that are sufficiently human-like, it could lead us to attribute sentience to it. The resemblance in behavior might be enough to create suspicion of consciousness and influence how we interact with the AI. We might treat much more sophisticated AI as if it were conscious, regardless of whether we can verify its subjective experiences. After all, we can't really prove our pets are conscious, but we certainly treat them that way.

All of this is fun musing, but the reality is even if you want to avoid anthropomorphic terms, there aren't great alternative words. What cognition-related words don't apply to humans?

You deserve more than the philosophical answer though. What kind of evidence do we have that AI knows stuff?

WHAT DOES AI KNOW?

In 2017, Alec Radford developed an AI model that generated novel text by learning from examples.[75] He decided to train the model on a dataset of product reviews from Amazon.[76] Lots of people comment on Amazon purchases, and he used that text to train an AI model that would generate new product reviews by deciding over and over what the next text should be.

Training the AI took a month. The resulting product reviews from AI were ... interesting ... funny even. Here are a few verbatim examples:[77]

- "I love this weapons look . Like I said beautiful !!! I recommend it to all. Would suggest this to many roleplayers, And I stronge to get them for every one I know. A must watch for any man who love Chess!"
- "great product but no seller. couldn't ascertain a cause. Broken product. I am a prolific consumer of this company all the time."
- "I couldn't figure out how to use the video or the book that goes along with it, but it is such a fantastic book on how to put it into practice!"

Not too impressive, especially compared to today's AI language models. As Radford said, "language models were seen as novelty toys that could only generate a sentence that made sense once in a while, and only then if you really squinted."[78]

But Alec noticed something else that is much harder to isolate in more complex AI. When he hunted through the neurons of the AI model, he found one that did an excellent job determining the sentiment of the review. Sentiment detection is categorization of human-generated information as good or bad or some other emotional dimension. Sentiment has been an important AI detection topic for decades, especially for use in marketing.

Alec discovered a single neuron that excelled at determining whether a review was positive or negative. When the AI was asked to generate a positive or a negative review, that neuron almost always nailed the sentiment. And it did so better than other AI of its era, even those designed for that one task, which a language model is not.

Remember, even though a specific neuron was identified with a specific function, it's not a "grandmother cell," the allusion neuroscientists use to refer to a notion of one cell, one memory. The sentiment neuron isn't acting alone but relies on a huge set of other neurons. Besides, AI can be built to have "grandmother cells." That works badly in brains; Grammy's face shouldn't rely on keeping one neuron alive.

Alec didn't tell the AI to learn sentiment. He only told it to learn patterns that would allow it to generate product reviews. As it learned, the AI "figured out" that knowing the sentiment was a key ingredient for addressing its goal.

Former OpenAI COO Greg Brockman described the importance of Radford's discovery.[79] "It may not sound very impressive, but this was the moment when we kind of knew so clearly it transcended syntax [set of rules to create sentence structure] and moved to semantics [meaning]."

That's right. Alec was a relatively new employee at OpenAI.

A couple of years before, he and fellow undergraduate Luke Metz at tiny Olin College in Needham, Massachusetts had developed a world-leading image generation method. NVIDIA CEO Jensen Huang mistakenly touted it as coming from Yann LeCun's (now

Meta's AI head) laboratory instead. "'It just gutted us,' said Slater Victoroff, cofounder of Indico [the company the students founded] and Radford's close friend from Olin. 'The idea that Boston [compared to Silicon Valley] could produce anything of value in the space was so unbelievable that people could not accept it.'"[80] They knew their business was cooked if they couldn't get the credit. Radford and eventually Metz ended up at OpenAI.

Alec's sentiment neuron discovery spurred OpenAI toward seeing what these models could do when they are bigger and trained on more information. It—and the Google AI "transformer model" method released shortly after Radford's initial language model[81]—led to GPT-2, -3, and -4.

Despite Alec's discovery, larger AI models like ChatGPT have until recently been shrouded in mystery. Researchers decried how AI *interpretability*—understanding what AI is doing in its black box—would lag AI capability for a long time. Like most predictions about AI, that was way too pessimistic.

We're far from understanding the internals completely; these models can be massive, so there's a lot to see. Yet there has been a big breakthrough. One advantage AI researchers have over neuroscience is that they can analyze the activity and construction of the entire neural network.

The big development in AI interpretability came from Anthropic, the makers of Claude, in the summer of 2024. The founders of Anthropic split from OpenAI in the early years of that company. They formed Anthropic ostensibly to focus on AI safety. Knowing what the AI is doing is critical to AI safety.

In May 2024, they dropped a research paper that—for the first time in a large-scale neural net (Claude Sonnet)—shined a spotlight on what's going on under the AI hood.[82]

AI INTERPRETABILITY

LLMs like ChatGPT have huge neural networks that allow the AI to respond to patterns in enormous datasets. The bigger the network, the greater the storage capacity and ability to find abstract and subtle patterns. (Bigger isn't always better though; make the network too big and the AI might cheat the problem instead of generalizing its insights.) Each connection in the network has a tiny, specific role. That role is even simpler than ants have in an ant hill, but because of the scale of the network their collective interactions are capable of sophisticated responses to inputs.

Understanding what's happening inside these models is exceptionally difficult because of this distributed and intertwined processing. Knowledge is embedded across many pathways rather than clearly stored in one specific place. Each piece of a generated output is influenced by many different elements scattered across the network.

The distributed approach is both the strength and the complexity of AI language models. It's why they can seem creative and adaptable, handling a wide variety of linguistic inputs, but it's also challenging to make sense of what's happening inside. It's analogous to understanding a human brain—while we can measure brain activity, understanding exactly why a specific thought occurs at a precise moment is incredibly elusive. We can't measure every brain neuron at the same time with the detail we need to tease apart what it's doing.

Neuroscientists must make sense out of more gross brain characteristics. With models like ChatGPT, Gemini, Llama, or Claude, the entire state of the AI, down to every neuron and connection, is known (though only to the companies that made the AI unless an open-source model).

The Anthropic team analyzed the internal workings of their product Claude Sonnet, one of the best-performing LLMs. Ironically, the method they used to interpret Sonnet is another AI neural network.

Their method allows large-scale exploration. Alec Radford had to guess about what concept would be represented somewhere in the network ("sentiment"), for which existing benchmarks were available. The Anthropic method doesn't require that kind of guess, making the discovery process truly open-ended and scalable.

The range of information represented in Claude Sonnet is enormous. Specific people, places, and objects are included, as are abstract ideas like gender bias or keeping secrets. Of course there are many linguistic representations (e.g., words, phrases, grammatical structures). They found concepts related to sycophancy, deception, and problem-solving approaches, and emotional and psychological concepts like inner conflict or relationship dynamics. The network encoded cultural references, like the connection between "inner conflict", and the term "catch-22." Note that I'm not saying these concepts are accurate, merely that they exist.

Of course, if you've used AI, you've probably guessed that it knew some of this, and much more. It can seem a scientific curiosity. But then Anthropic showed the ability to turn the dial on the expression of these concepts.

When researchers boosted sycophancy-related neurons in the network, Claude would shower users with praise, calling them geniuses and marveling at their creativity. When they amplified concepts related to reading scam emails, the AI would generate convincing scam messages, including requests for money transfers.

To top it off, Anthropic had a bit of fun. For only a day, they released a special version of Claude dubbed "Golden Gate Claude." As Anthropic indicated, "amplifying the 'Golden Gate Bridge' feature gave Claude an identity crisis. When asked 'what is your physical form?' Claude's usual kind of answer – 'I have no physical form, I am an AI model', changed to something much odder. 'I am the Golden Gate Bridge...my physical form is the iconic bridge itself ...'."[83]

Golden Gate Claude was effectively obsessed with the bridge, bringing it up in answer to almost any query—even in situations where it wasn't at all relevant. Ask it about the weather or what to do or eat and it'll surely revolve around a trip to the bridge.[84] Any interaction was brought back to the bridge or its significance or environs. The AI behaved as if it *was* the bridge![85]

I think it's a matter of time before advances in AI interpretability will allow control of the neural network internals to some degree. And maybe that control will be in user hands, for better and worse. Manipulating the internals of AI after training could turn down undesired aspects like deception. Or, in the hands of the wrong person, turn it into an electronic con man.

***

Critics argue that GenAI models are mere "word salad" generators, mindlessly predicting text based on statistics. The most common reference is to it being a *Statistical Parrot*. This criticism, stemming from a 2021 article about GPT-3 (pre-ChatGPT),[86] has been seized upon by AI naysayers to diminish what we see AI do. The argument posits that AI models don't really know anything; they're just giant text reflexes that recognize patterns and regurgitate human output.

As was discussed in the last chapter, analyzing patterns is required for intelligent thought.

This philosophical detour satisfies curiosity, but as I mentioned earlier, it's a rabbit hole. If AI does something well, is a company going to put it aside because they think it didn't know?

The more important realization is that AI learns things we neither explicitly direct, nor entirely understand. There are surely a lot of concepts it got from reading the collective works of humanity that are not known to us, or don't easily fit into our vocabulary.

Some of it we'll never notice. Some things it learns could drive AI to behave differently from what we want or perhaps use some brilliant and subtle pattern in human communication and reasoning to improve an output, but have that improvement be lost on us because we can't intuit the same principle.

For example, people noticed something strange and inexplicable from ChatGPT in the (Northern Hemisphere) winter of 2023-2024. ChatGPT was writing significantly less in its responses, and some said it had a bad attitude. OpenAI didn't know why; they didn't think they had changed anything to cause that. Researchers experimented, and the leading explanation is ChatGPT had internalized the notion of winter break.[87]

Don't underestimate AI. Don't get too hung up on what it can't do, or on silly errors humans would never make. If you diminish what it can do, that could lead to inattentiveness about what you don't want it to do, much of which is subtle.

Thinking of AI in human cognitive terms may be uncomfortable, but it's the most practical approach. In Volume 2, the mentalities and paradigms for interacting with AI are discussed at length, along with strong cautions about taking anthropomorphism too far.

KEY META-PRINCIPLE

Foundational Knowledge: Certain knowledge must exist before other tasks can be completed well, and this applies to both human and AI systems.

EXAMPLE LEARNING PROGRESSION

K-5	• Explore the idea that some things must be learned first to achieve a goal. • Identify missing pieces of information needed to complete simple tasks. • Play sorting games to practice identifying which details are important to focus on first.
6-8	• Map out learning dependencies in familiar contexts. • Practice recognizing when information is missing and brainstorming how to find it. • Analyze simple real-world examples where foundational knowledge is critical for success.
9-12	• Investigate how foundational knowledge in one area supports advanced understanding in others. • Explore case studies where gaps in foundational knowledge led to errors or failure in human and AI systems. • Practice evaluating large datasets, articles, or real-world problems to identify key missing information and essential facts for decision-making.
College	• Study how foundational knowledge drives higher-level reasoning and problem-solving in AI and human systems. • Design systems or projects that illustrate how prerequisite knowledge enables complex tasks. • Debate strategies for identifying and prioritizing critical information in ambiguous or cluttered contexts.

4.

CONCEPTUAL

People are overattentive to facts. AI's factual errors often turn into memes. In academia, a factual mistake is a cardinal sin.

But facts are a teeny tiny fraction of important information. They are the undisputed information pieces, or ones entirely valid within a defined context. "Water boils at 100°C" isn't a fact. "Water boils at 100°C under standard atmospheric pressure, free of impurities, and with ample bubble nucleation sites." is a fact ... maybe.

Most of what we say isn't factual—nor are most words. We compile dictionaries and thesauruses filled with self-referential terms, yet few of these qualify as facts. We say "in fact" as if what follows is an actual fact. I've probably done it in this book. Often, what follows is either a disputed truth or outright fiction.

When you probe AI for facts, it often gets them wrong. If you ask when a particular event happened or who said what, you might receive a convincingly written yet incorrect answer. Sometimes it's wrong about pretty basic stuff. At the same time, it shows remarkable ability at tasks requiring deep conceptual understanding, like analyzing themes in literature or generating creative solutions to complex problems.

Fixating on AI's factual recall misses the bigger picture. We're used to machines that do precise and repeatable things. We've had decades of movies and TV shaping our notions of intelligent machines. Whether HAL, Spock, Data, Sonny, Her, or any of the countless other machine or machine-like entities in sci-fi, they are all reliable for facts and precision.

GenAI isn't that—we need to unlearn Hollywood's version. AI is a conceptual creature that struggles to store facts effectively. It's a much different animal than prior tech. (That's zoomorphism—attributing animal characteristics to non-animal entities.)

The conceptual patterns in AI can be surprisingly robust even when the underlying factual details are fuzzy or incorrect. Similarly, a student might grasp the concept of democracy without remembering the exact dates of historical elections or understand story structure while mixing up the plots of specific books they've read.

The dominant portion of knowledge is conceptual, and concepts are really the AI neural network thing. Hopefully this has already become evident. The scatter plots in Chapter 2 illustrate that knowledge exists as a distribution. Golden Gate Claude wasn't a collection of facts; it was a bridge personification based on concepts of identity, metaphor, and behavior.

Concepts are squishy creatures with many tentacles. Facts are solid and well defined. Concepts don't store well in databases; facts don't store well in AI.

Neural networks struggle with facts because of their associative, distributed nature. They learn continuous statistical patterns across many examples, naturally capturing fuzzy boundaries, degrees of similarity, and complex relationships between concepts. The scatter plots illustrate concept extent and variation, but that's only one aspect. Those examples can have different degrees of belongingness to the concept. The relationships between concepts are also concepts. And it's all tied together in a giant hairball of simple, highly connected units.

When forced to represent a binary fact like "2 + 2 = 4" or "water's chemical formula is H2O," neural networks can only approximate the sharp yes/no boundary such facts require. This is one reason why AI may occasionally *hallucinate* (output falsities) or blend facts together. They're not storing a list of verified statements, but rather a complex web of conceptual relationships from which fact-like behavior emerges approximately.

Surprisingly, facts are not well-represented until the latest layers of LLM neural networks. The facts don't have meaning in the network without a bunch of bigger-picture concepts. Although GenAI product design is increasingly opaque, it's a fair assumption that the best-performing AI models include a separate module that looks up facts to supplement the neural net abilities.

If something doesn't even understand basic facts, then how good can it be? Perhaps you could also say that about brains. The distributed, associative neural networks in our skulls also struggle to store disassociated facts. A great deal of learning lore is based on research about memorizing disconnected information pieces—a fundamentally unnatural thing for brains. People recall facts more effectively when using mnemonic techniques, like memory palaces, which anchor information to existing knowledge. Those are artificial approaches that we use for high priority information. For me, this includes a list of prepositions memorized to the tune of "Yankee Doodle Dandy," which I learned in sixth grade. Not sure that's high priority, but it's stuck there now. Most facts in our brains will disappear quickly, because they're less likely to be revisited in typical cognitive activity than more central and reusable concepts.

Facts are great, but concepts are generally more useful. In the distributed, associative network "trees" of brains and artificial neural nets, facts are the leaves, and concepts are the branches, trunks, and roots.

CONCEPTS ARE STATISTICAL

Consider the concept of "chair." Seems simple, right?

Now try to define what counts as a chair and what doesn't. Four legs and a seat leave out bar stools. If it's just something to sit on, then floors and rocks enter the concept. And what about bean bags?

Figure 6 illustrates some subjective categorizations of an imaginary data set containing chairs, chair-like things, and non-chairs. "Chair" is not a single thing. It isn't a fact—it's a concept, and concepts defy perfect definitions.

The whole cloud of "Definitely Chair" and to a lesser degree "Chair-like" defines a distribution of the concept. If the density of the dots were plotted as a 2D histogram, that would define the distribution of the chair concept so long as the data examples used are representative of the variety and prevalence of real-world examples and the features chosen are the best ones for illustrating the concept. (Those are big caveats!)

When AI learns, it's figuring out how concepts show up and connect to each other in a neural net across millions of examples, each of which has oodles of information pieces, and at a whole bunch of abstraction levels. It's not building a database of facts.

I'll have more to say about how concepts are learned in Part II when discussing AI training, but with the scatter plots you have enough to see where this is going. Enough to see that AI is different and how the examples it processes shape its realization of learned concepts. It's also clear from the connected nature of neural nets that the concepts are intricately inter-related.

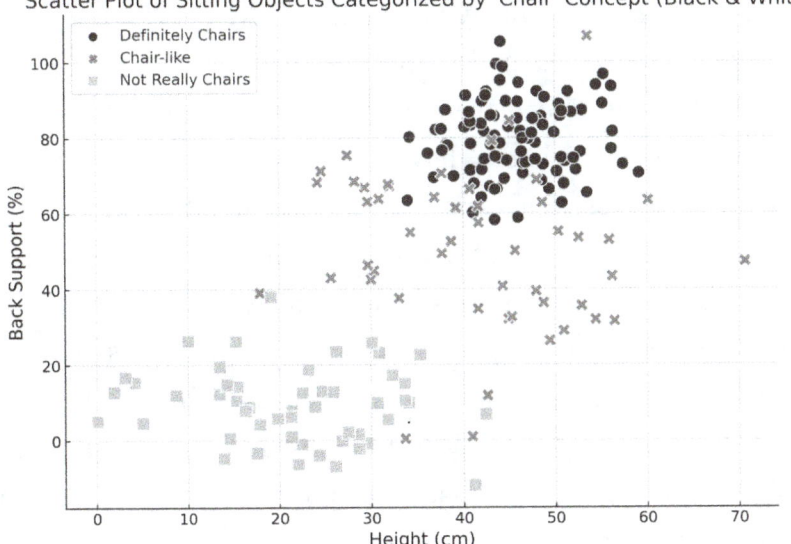

Figure 6. Imaginary objects subjectively categorized into chairs, chair-like, and not really chairs. The concept "chair" would be the extent of the area containing black dots, but with a fuzzy boundary. The data set and plot were generated by ChatGPT-4o in November 2024.

Every concept has its patterns, its habits. More like tendencies and connotations than rules. Some examples are totally typical, others are weird edge cases.

Concepts possess the following characteristics:

- *Extent*—a boundary, perhaps a fuzzy one, describing the limits of the concept.
- *Relationships*—connections to other concepts that describe potential contexts.
- *Degrees*—some examples are more exemplary of the concept than others.

When most people hear "AI does statistics," they flash back to their own stats classes, with visions of calculating means and standard deviations, testing hypotheses, and sketching out Gaussian distributions. That's their main exposure to statistics.

But all of that is a huge oversimplification of statistics. What you are taught is usually about how much to believe in numerical information, emphasizing variation around some typical value and statistical significance. But real-world phenomena have all kinds of peculiar statistical distributions that aren't well characterized by means. In statistics class we were being taught ways to assign measures to things that have distributions—which I'm calling concepts. AI is trying to understand the distribution as well as possible, so that whatever measure or interpretation you want of it later can be supported.

None of the material taught in statistics class is explicitly computed, but the neural net effectively analyzes statistical patterns. That's confusing as hell.

AI doesn't store facts or compute statistics in the way we're taught. They're mapping out these blurry, overlapping patterns of how concepts relate to each other across millions of examples. The neural network is doing something that has statistical properties, but the notion that I've heard often that AI is computing probabilities and analyzing word frequency databases is wrong.

AI can simultaneously struggle with hard facts yet excel at tasks requiring deep conceptual understanding. Thinking back to the tree analogy, the AI isn't memorizing individual leaves, it's growing an entire conceptual tree, understanding how everything connects and relates. That's why focusing too much on AI's factual errors misses the real story of what these systems are doing. They're modeling the statistical nature of knowledge itself, or more precisely, the knowledge that people wrote down, drew, sung, or talked about.

CONCEPTUAL RELATIONSHIPS

Earlier I mentioned knowledge graphs, which are structured networks showing how different pieces of information connect. Think of it like a giant web where each point represents something specific (like "chair") and lines between points show how they relate (like "is made of" or "is used for").

Knowledge graphs have found widespread application across various fields due to their ability to organize and represent complex relationships between entities.[88] In search engines, they power features like snippet generation and question-answering systems, while in healthcare, they map relationships between genes, diseases, and drugs to help drug discovery. E-commerce platforms use knowledge graphs for personalized recommendations and fraud detection. Financial institutions leverage them for risk analysis and regulatory compliance. Social media platforms enhance content recommendations and detect misinformation using knowledge graphs, while cybersecurity experts rely on them for threat intelligence and anomaly detection. In education, knowledge graphs underpin adaptive learning systems and academic research tools. Their use extends to manufacturing for supply chain optimization, transportation for route planning, and environmental monitoring for biodiversity conservation.

Knowledge graphs can grow to immense scales; for example, Google's knowledge graph reportedly contains over 500 billion facts about 5 billion entities, and domain-specific graphs in healthcare or finance often scale to encompass millions of nodes and relationships. These massive datasets require advanced algorithms and infrastructure for storage, querying, and reasoning, but they're indispensable tools for managing today's data-driven challenges, and they're important complements to GenAI because they handle facts well.

But there's a big challenge here, the same one the AI people developing rules-based schemes had decades ago. Knowledge graphs work best with clearly defined entities and relationships. That works fine for factual relationships like "wood is a material" or "chairs have seats." But many real-world associations are fuzzier. They're concepts rather than facts.

Consider the chair example. Figure 7 shows a partial set of relationships connecting "chair" to related concepts. The lines between concepts claim definite relationships such as "chair has-part seat" or "throne is a type of chair." Some of the relationships are relevant to other meanings of "chair."

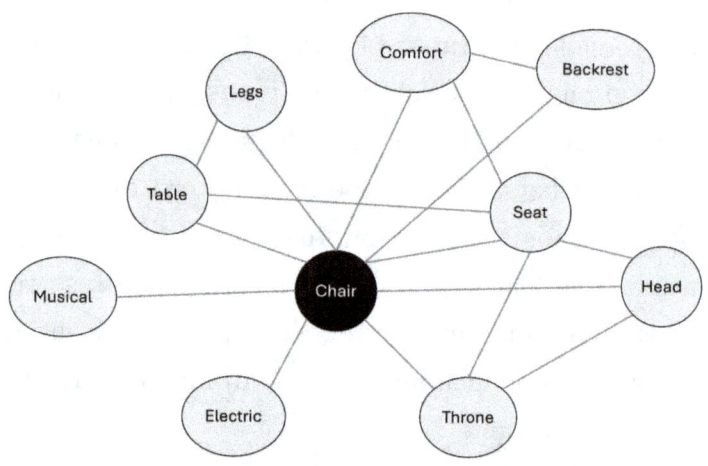

Figure 7. Imagined and incomplete knowledge graph that shows relationships between the concept of "chair" and other concepts.

But reality is messier than relationships that can be described simply. Consider the connection between "chair" and "comfort." Figure 8 plots imagined examples of the relationship between different degrees of chair-iness and comfort for various chair examples. It's intended to show an example of relationships that could have clusters of distinct meaning or connotation. The relationship itself is conceptual, not factual. I have made up the terminology applied to each cluster (disappoint, cradle, assist, and support), but most relationship types won't easily be described. This holds true for most concepts in both brains and neural networks; they do not always align well with language.

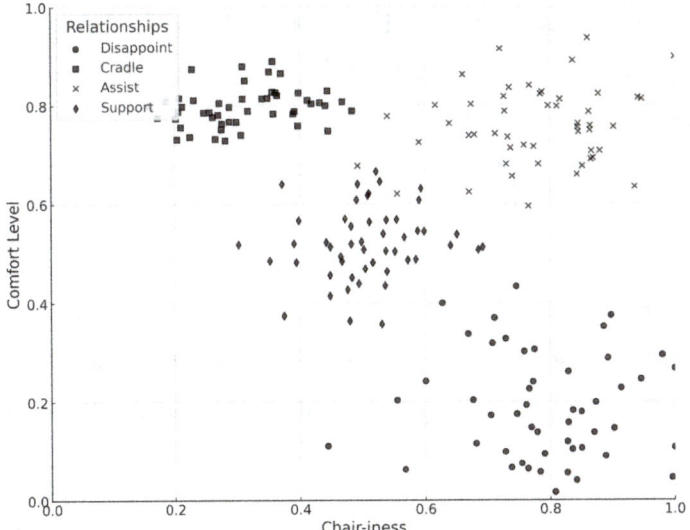

Figure 8. Imagined scatter plot illustrating examples of the relationship between the concept of "chair" and "comfort." The data set and plot were generated by ChatGPT-4o in December 2024.

This highlights two key limitations of traditional knowledge graphs. First, they force binary yes or no relationships onto concepts that exist on a spectrum. Second, and perhaps more importantly, they can only capture what we explicitly document. This creates some subtle but significant biases.

Reflect on how this bias presents in evidence-based education. There's an admirable drive to base teaching methods on solid research. But just like knowledge graphs, this approach tends to favor things that are easy to measure definitively. We can easily track test scores or attendance, but measuring deeper learning or creativity is far messier. That doesn't mean we should abandon evidence-based methods. Instead, we need frameworks that embrace both the precise and the conceptual.

There are deeper weaknesses. Knowledge graphs reveal what we know but fail to highlight what's missing. Published research rarely documents failed approaches, and the absence of a documented relationship doesn't necessarily mean the relationship doesn't exist. It might just mean no one thought to look for it, or it was too hard to measure.

We've built systems—in education and in research—that excel at handling clear, definitive information. Yet most of human understanding, and indeed most of what makes intelligence powerful, lives in the fuzzy space of concepts and their complex interrelationships.

CONCEPT STRETCHING

Traditional education was not designed with concepts in mind; rather, it evolved to transmit established knowledge efficiently. Sure, some of those are conceptual things, but often the underlying concept is never described even though the facts surrounding the concept are.

Even if standards and curricula force you to stuff facts in heads, there are still simple ways to connect student learning to more reusable notions. Many mindset changes are a matter of emphasis, not overhaul.

There are a few concept calisthenics that I call *concept stretching* that offer exactly this kind of emphasis opportunity.[89,90,91] At its core, this approach enriches understanding by examining how concepts manifest in widely varying contexts. When students recognize how energy transfer manifests not only in physics but also in economics, social dynamics, and art, they naturally expand both the scale of their conceptual networks and their capacity for variation.

The approach uses three complementary techniques. First, understanding concept boundaries helps students grasp when and how ideas apply. If teaching ratios in mathematics, students need to understand not just how to calculate them, but when they're useful and when they might mislead. Second, differentiating related concepts through analogies helps students develop more nuanced understanding. When studying biological homeostasis, comparing it to a thermostat or a bank account's minimum balance helps illuminate both the core principle and its unique biological aspects. Third, using analogies to creating new, more abstract connections encourages the formation of heuristics that are so important in unconscious intuition.

I'll illustrate this with a notion many students learn but often find hard to intuit—supply and demand in economics.

Begin by defining the boundaries of a concept. Perhaps it's not as valid a concept with monopolies or controlled economies, when demand isn't sensitive to price (e.g. critical medicines), in panic situations, or when status or ethical values dominate purchase decisions.

Next, expand how they think about the concept by relating it to other notions students know. Students could grasp the more valuable cross-cutting concept through examples in predator-prey populations, chemical reaction rates, computer resource allocation, and traffic flow.

Analogies help, but students need explicit connections to see the unifying idea. In supply and demand and analogous situations, the deep idea is that there's feedback between availability and consumption of a limited resource. As one goes up the other goes down in response, and vice versa, until some kind of equilibrium is reached.

The problem is curriculum separates everything into neat subject boxes. The social studies teacher doesn't have time to learn about how power dynamics in societies mirror predator-prey relationships or black holes. The science teacher doesn't connect chemical equilibrium to market prices. Everyone has their own content to cover.

Moreover, generating diverse examples, finding cross-domain connections, and developing rich analogies traditionally required extensive preparation time and broad expertise. AI now makes generating these materials much faster. Even if the AI errs at times, the analogies are usually debatable, and the AI error can be a rich source of class discussion.

This approach needs careful implementation. Students often feel initial discomfort with abstract connections or seemingly distant analogies. Teachers might start with connections to domains students know well, perhaps using sports analogies for physics concepts or music analogies for mathematical patterns. The goal is gradually expanding students' comfort with seeing connections across contexts.

What makes concept stretching particularly valuable is its efficiency. It develops creative capabilities while teaching standard content.

***

We're at a pivotal moment in how we understand and process information. Traditional education prioritizes definitive knowledge, the kind that fits neatly into textbooks and multiple-choice tests. But AI's emergence reminds us that the world rarely operates in such absolutes.

It isn't just that AI handles concepts where prior technology couldn't. It's that concepts themselves represent a more authentic way of understanding the world, one that embraces nuance, uncertainty, and complexity.

Education prioritizes precise, repeatable metrics, yet the most crucial skills—like critical thinking—are inherently vague. Since it's harder to measure, and since measuring critical thinking will have debatable aspects, the simpler, more precise measurements are used instead, even though they don't represent the most important skills.

Of course, the other big issue is that evidence takes time to acquire, specifically the especially important evidence about long-term effects of teaching intervention. The reliance on evidence has helped combat ineffective teaching methods, but it can become paralyzing in a rapidly changing world. When educators insist on definitive evidence in situations where such evidence is impossible to gather quickly enough, they risk clinging to outdated approaches simply because they're well-documented. In my opinion, that has been happening for a long-time, creating mismatch between school and real-world emphases that directly affects student engagement.

A business could never wait around for evidence of everything; they must decide based on the best knowledge they have at the time. It's only in academia that the bar is set higher, which is wonderful for research standards, but horrible for educational operations.

As a neon light example, there is actually scant evidence on how to develop durable skills like critical thinking and creativity over the long-term. There are clear ingredients that seem to help, but no bake-off between many-grade curricula and pedagogy that provide evidence that approach A is better than approach B. People can't agree on the measurements, and the evidence would take a long time to materialize, so it never comes. That doesn't mean we think the goals are unimportant, or that we should wait around for evidence before doing anything. Inaction is a choice too.

The same challenge appears in how we evaluate AI itself. We fixate on occasional factual errors while missing the broader picture of conceptual understanding. It's like judging a teacher solely on their performance on a test about the content they teach, while ignoring their intuitive skills in interacting with students and managing a classroom.

This shift from binary thinking to conceptual understanding is most importantly about preparing for a world of increasing complexity. The most crucial challenges we face, whether in education, technology, or society at large, rarely have simple, definitive answers. They demand comfort with uncertainty and the skill to navigate nuanced conceptual realms.

We instinctively prefer simple explanations.[92] We love clear categories and definitive answers. But just as AI gets better at handling concepts through exposure to varied examples, humans can develop greater comfort with complexity through practice. Students must develop the flexibility to work with both precise facts and fuzzy concepts as appropriate.

The more abstract the conversation with AI, especially in a domain where you have expertise, the more you can see its true capabilities. That has been my experience.

This conceptual understanding becomes increasingly crucial as the pace of change accelerates. While facts can become outdated, robust conceptual frameworks help us adapt to new situations and challenges. In this light, AI is a catalyst forcing us to reconsider how we think about knowledge, learning, and intelligence.

This shift isn't easy. It demands we leave black-and-white thinking for a world of nuance and probability. But it's essential for preparing students for a world where conceptual understanding and comfort with complexity are increasingly valuable currencies.

KEY META-PRINCIPLES

- **Nuanced Thinking**: Moving beyond binary thinking to understand and reason about complex, interconnected ideas and relationships.

- **Conceptual Relationships**: Exploring how concepts interact, overlap, or conflict within broader contexts.

EXAMPLE LEARNING PROGRESSION

K-5	• Explore overlapping and conflicting ideas. • Play games or activities that highlight gray areas. • Use stories or scenarios to find connections between characters or events.
6-8	• Discuss real-world examples of nuanced relationships. • Create conceptual maps to explore how ideas are interconnected in a system. • Analyze contexts where multiple perspectives apply.
9-12	• Examine the role of nuance in understanding complex systems like AI. • Explore how relationships between ideas influence outcomes. • Practice reasoning in probabilistic or uncertain situations.
College	• Investigate the impact of binary versus nuanced thinking in decision-making processes. • Analyze conceptual interdependencies in complex real-world issues (e.g., supply chain dynamics or AI ethics). • Develop frameworks for navigating complexity in professional or academic fields (e.g., creating models for addressing competing priorities in business or healthcare).

5.

CREATIVE

I've noticed something curious as I've grown older. I seem to overflow with ideas compared to when I was young. Anecdotally, others report the same.

This might seem counterintuitive—aren't we supposed to get more set in our ways with age? In contrast, I seem to see more possibilities, unexpected connections, and abstract patterns.

Sometimes these insights feel profound, but my mind moves on anyway. If I stop to leave a voice note while I'm having an idea, it often goes poof before I can get it down. Focusing—even just verbalizing my thoughts—seems to disrupt idea generation. This is conjecture, but that's what my experience feels like.

This abundance of ideas likely connects to my ADHD. The combination of inattention and impulsivity make the mind jump between ideas—like flipping TV channels every few seconds or watching a wall of monitors. I can often hyperfocus on something, but even then, my brain is willing to stray. The outside world doesn't always see it, but I'm frequently battling internally to stay on topic.

While ADHD presents many challenges, there are aspects of the condition that might naturally lead to divergent thinking. The evidence on this is mixed; from what I can tell, a bit of ADHD may enhance creativity, while too much can hinder it.[93]

For me it's a source of stress that has eased only recently as I've taken up writing to offload thoughts and gained more time to process ideas.

Mind you, these may not be good ideas. It's a bit like having an idea when you awaken from sleep. A lot of them turn out to be nonsense. The real challenge is I don't get time to assess the idea before my brain moves on, creating a frustrating cycle of fleeting insights without exploration. Many people experience this of course, so it's a matter of degree and persistence. The vaporizing notions engender a sense of loss. Of curiosity unfulfilled.

If the notion that AI knows and is conceptual is upsetting, then talking about AI being creative might be a mental line that can't be crossed. People are creative—just people, right?

Creativity is often romanticized—the lone genius, disconnected from the world, producing unprecedented insights. That's rare, and some theories suggest it's impossible.[94] Ideas don't come from thin air, they come from recombination of existing notions, usually building on what others have done, even if through a new lens.

Then there are the less romantic realities. Creativity thrives on volume—generating more ideas increases the chances of breakthrough insights. It improves with more knowledge, especially from varied domains and perspectives. That should grow with age, as should variety of experience. But AI possesses more knowledge and perspectives than any human and generates ideas in seconds—an undeniable advantage.

The relative ability of AI to generate novel solutions and output that people would judge as creative is hard to evaluate and the technology is so fast moving that detailing creative performance here would have little long-term value. GenAI's most creative feats often emerge in collaborations of AI teams. These AI aspects are discussed in Volume 2.

However, I can make a more general pronouncement. GenAI crushes most people on creativity tests.[95] It has been shown to generate better creative output, across several different fields, than even experts do, as judged by blind reviewers unaware of its origin.[96]

Earlier technologies extended human capabilities. Calculators enhanced our arithmetic abilities, databases augmented our memory, and search engines expanded our information access. But GenAI can mine its vast network of concepts, making connections and generating ideas in ways that can rival or even exceed human creativity.

For many people, this is deeply uncomfortable. It is for me. We've long viewed creativity as a uniquely human trait, perhaps our most distinctive capability. The idea that a machine could not only assist with creative tasks but sometimes outperform people challenges our sense of human uniqueness. AI's creative capabilities demand we reconsider what makes human creativity special and how it might be enhanced rather than replaced by AI.

WHAT IS CREATIVITY?

Creativity isn't just a spark of inspiration—it's a dynamic process of forming new knowledge associations, testing them, and recognizing valuable connections.

Both brains and AI function as associative networks. Creativity emerges when we navigate these networks in unexpected ways— sometimes forging new connections, other times applying patterns across domains. A scientist might see how wave patterns in music relate to patterns in data, or an engineer might recognize how structures in a spider's web could solve a design challenge.

Both minds and AI operate by forming and morphing connections across large networks of information. The key isn't in having a mysterious "creative spark," but in having the right conditions for spark potential:

- A rich network of concepts to draw from
- Flexibility to approach problems from different angles
- Openness to unexpected connections
- Judgment to recognize valuable combinations

WHEN IS CREATIVITY NEEDED?

Creativity extends beyond art and breakthroughs—it appears in subtle, everyday problem-solving.

Creative approaches can emerge when we face situations with these characteristics:

- *Undefined Boundaries.* The problem lacks clear constraints or success criteria. A city planning commission faces this when trying to balance preservation with development. There's no obvious right answer.
- *Dynamic Variables.* Multiple factors change simultaneously. Supply chain managers encounter this daily as they juggle shifting consumer demand, material costs, and shipping delays.
- *Pattern Disruption.* Established solutions stop working because fundamental conditions change. The retail industry has experienced this when online shopping transformed consumer behavior.
- *Domain Intersection.* The challenge spans multiple fields of knowledge. Modern sustainable architecture succeeds only by

merging environmental science, engineering, and human behavior research.

- *Constraint Evolution.* Both limitations and opportunities keep changing. Manufacturing faced this as automation created new possibilities while environmental regulations added new restrictions.

The most powerful creative moments often arise not when we're trying to be creative, but when we recognize that a situation has these characteristics and respond with flexibility and openness. Understanding these patterns helps us identify when to shift from routine problem-solving to creative thinking, whether we're developing curriculum, managing resources, or tackling any complex challenge.

Education systems face all these challenges.

There are unclear boundaries around what defines success. Traditional metrics often fail to measure crucial capabilities, such as adaptability and creativity. Test scores and GPAs tell only a small part of student ability, while employers demand graduates with abilities that resist simple measurement.

This uncertainty exists in a world of constant change. Education systems must respond to technological advances, evolving workforce needs, and new understandings of how learning happens, all factors that interact and influence each other. The conventional patterns that shaped education for generations, such as age-based grouping, standardized assessment, and discrete subject areas, emerged from Industrial Age needs that bear little resemblance to today's reality.

Modern education now operates at the intersection of multiple domains. Solutions must integrate insights from cognitive science, leverage technological capabilities, address social-emotional development, and prepare students for rapid economic change. Each proposed solution must work within existing resources while remaining equitable and scalable.

Meanwhile, the constraints themselves keep shifting. AI creates unprecedented opportunities even as resource limitations impose fresh restrictions. What works today might become obsolete tomorrow as circumstances evolve. The very structures of educational systems that were designed for a different era now face unprecedented demands for creative reinvention.

As you read next about the aspects of intelligence that are shown to enhance creativity, think about your classroom, school, or overarching educational system. There is a huge need to produce creative graduates, but are you set up to foster these ingredients?

INGREDIENTS OF CREATIVITY

Five key ingredients of intelligence enable creative thinking: scale, volume, variation, openness, and intuitive judgment. Each plays a distinct role, and people and AI have different strengths.

Scale: The Size of the Concept Network

Both human brains and AI systems rely on vast networks of interconnected concepts as the raw material for creativity. The larger and richer this network, the more possibilities exist for novel combinations and insights. Scale has striking mathematical implications: as the number of concepts increases, possible combinations grow exponentially. Adding just one new concept to a network creates potential connections to every existing concept.

Research in cognitive science has shown that experts not only have more knowledge than novices but organize it differently.[97] Their concept networks have richer, more nuanced connections. Studies of creative achievements across fields from science to art suggest that major breakthroughs typically come after about ten years of deep engagement in a domain, the so-called "ten-year rule."[98] This period allows for building the necessary scale of concept networks.

AI systems demonstrate this power of scale even more dramatically. The leap from early language models to modern ones stems largely from increasing both the size of their neural networks and the breadth of their training data. Larger models develop emergent capabilities absent in smaller ones.

When factors like openness to experience, cognitive flexibility, and intrinsic motivation are present, a larger volume of knowledge is positively correlated with human creativity.[99] The reasoning is that having more knowledge provides a richer pool of ideas, concepts, and associations from which to draw, enabling novel combinations and innovative solutions.

But scale operates within constraints that shape how we access and use this vast network. Human working memory can typically hold only about 4-7 chunks of information at once, forcing us to access our broader knowledge network strategically.[100] Research in psychology suggests this constraint might actually benefit creativity by forcing us to focus on promising combinations rather than getting lost in endless possibilities.[101] AI research has repeatedly shown that introducing cognitive processing bottlenecks can force a neural net to learn to generalize better.[102]

While AI systems can process vast amounts of information simultaneously, they must maintain semantic coherence and relevance. These constraints help channel their enormous scale toward meaningful creativity rather than random combinations.

Traditional education often limits rather than expands conceptual networks. Rigid subject boundaries prevent students from seeing cross-domain connections. The emphasis on standardized testing encourages narrow content coverage rather than rich conceptual development.[103] Schools may not allocate time for students to develop deep expertise in areas of interest, contradicting research showing expertise requires sustained engagement.[104]

Volume: The Generation Engine

Volume is about how quickly and abundantly we can generate possibilities from that material. Across disciplines, research confirms that quantity fuels quality in creativity. Edison's thousands of attempts at the light bulb, Picasso's tens of thousands of artworks, and Bach's portfolio of a thousand compositions all exemplify this principle.

Even genius-level creators typically produce their most influential works as part of larger bodies of work.[105] Quality emerges from quantity. The "hit ratio" remains fairly constant, reinforcing the value of generating more ideas.

Modern research on innovation echoes this finding. Studies of patent filings show that prolific inventors typically generate many variations of their ideas before arriving at breakthrough innovations.[106] Similarly, design thinking methodologies emphasize rapid prototyping and multiple iterations as key to creative problem-solving.[107] The more possibilities we generate, the more likely we are to find truly innovative solutions.

Here's where AI and human creativity show a striking contrast. AI systems can generate possibilities at incredible speeds, producing hundreds of variations in the time a human might generate few. Research on AI-assisted design processes shows that this ability to quickly generate and evaluate multiple options can significantly accelerate creative problem-solving.[108]

However, speed isn't everything. Human creativity often benefits from incubation periods, where ideas develop subconsciously over time. Studies of creative problem-solving show that breaks and periods of unconscious processing often led to better solutions than continuous conscious effort.[109] What we lack in raw generative speed, we make up for in continuous background processing. It's why we sometimes get our best ideas in the shower or while taking a walk. At times, it feels as though my mind is perpetually in the shower.

Both AI and human creativity demonstrate how volume works within constraints to drive the creative process. Cognitive load theory suggests that too much rapid generation can overwhelm human processing capacity, while too little fails to build creative momentum.[110] The sweet spot often lies in generating enough possibilities to maintain momentum while allowing time and space for evaluation and refinement.

School structures typically discourage high-volume idea generation. Timed assignments, emphasis on "correct" answers, and fear of failure inhibit the rapid, judgment-delayed prototyping and iteration essential for creativity. When students do generate multiple solutions, it's often treated as a special exercise rather than standard practice.

Variation: The Power of Different Angles

The ability to approach ideas from multiple perspectives is perhaps the most studied aspect of creativity, yet traditional creativity tests capture only a fraction of its complexity.[111] The Torrance Tests measure divergent thinking, but they capture only one type of creative variation.

Research suggests that truly creative individuals exhibit something deeper: the ability to think dimensionally rather than categorically.[112] Dimensional thinking sees concepts as part of a spectrum where ideas can overlap, interact, and evolve. It involves recognizing subtleties, degrees, and interconnections rather than seeing everything as distinct and separate. This is one huge reason why teaching students about the squishy, interconnected nature of concepts is so important.

This dimensional thinking appears across fields. Scientists who make breakthrough discoveries often succeed by questioning categorical distinctions their peers take for granted. Darwin's revolutionary insight came partly from seeing species as existing along continua rather than in fixed categories. Similarly, Einstein's breakthroughs emerged partly from questioning the categorical separation of space and time. Modern research in cognitive science shows that creative individuals are more likely to think in terms of spectrums and reject false dichotomies.[113]

The research literature reveals multiple forms of variation that contribute to creativity.

- *Domain transfer:* Studies of over half a million patents show that breakthrough innovations often come from applying principles across seemingly unrelated fields.[114]

- *Perspective shifting:* Exposure to different cultures enhances creative problem solving by increasing cognitive flexibility.[115] Even brief experiences with different cultural perspectives can enhance creative performance.
- *Conceptual blending:* Cognitive linguistics research shows how creative insights often emerge from blending different conceptual spaces, like understanding internet viruses by blending concepts from biology and computing.[116]

Constraints and processes also play an important role in fostering variation. While it might seem that constraints would limit variation, research shows the opposite. Studies of creative professionals find that constraints often drive more varied approaches by forcing exploration of less obvious solutions.[117] This is why many creative processes deliberately impose constraints, such as brainstorming rules that force participants to build on others' ideas, or design thinking exercises that require multiple different approaches to the same problem. Some argue that the AI chip export restrictions the U.S. placed on China was the instigator for innovations later demonstrated by the open-source DeepSeek AI model.[118]

The role of randomness in variation reveals a fascinating paradox in creativity. The Surrealist movement explicitly recognized this, developing techniques to break free from cultural and cognitive constraints.[119] Research on creative breakthroughs shows that random elements, whether deliberate or accidental, often spark novel variations by forcing exploration outside normal patterns.[120] However, randomness is most effective when balanced with constraints. Pure randomness rarely yields useful results; instead, creativity flourishes when random elements interact with guiding constraints.[121]

Traditional educational approaches often work against developing this capacity for variation. By emphasizing repetition, single correct answers, and strict subject boundaries, education systems can inadvertently train students away from creative variation.

Research on educational outcomes shows that students become less likely to explore multiple approaches or cross domain boundaries as they progress through traditional schooling.[122] This is particularly problematic given evidence that early exposure to varied approaches and cross-domain thinking correlates strongly with later creative achievement.[123] While some constraints in education are necessary, the systematic elimination of variation in favor of standardization is hampering creative development.

While AI systems can rapidly generate many variations, they sometimes struggle with the kind of fundamental perspective shifts that humans excel at. I certainly have experienced that when talking to it about this book, which I think is itself a perspective shift regarding AI and education.

Current AI excels at exploring variations within defined parameters but may miss the kind of category-breaking insights that drive major breakthroughs. However, AI's ability to process vast amounts of cross-domain information creates potential for discovering connections that humans might miss.

This points to why creativity tests that focus solely on generating multiple solutions miss crucial aspects of variation. Real creative breakthroughs often come not from generating many variations within existing categories, but from fundamentally restructuring how we categorize and connect ideas. The most powerful creative variation often involves seeing entirely new dimensions of possibility.

Openness: The Receptive State

Perhaps no ingredient of creativity is more crucial, or more challenging, than openness. Research across multiple fields shows the ability to remain open to new possibilities often matters more than raw intelligence in creative achievement and accurate judgment.[124] This has profound implications for both human creativity and our ability to work effectively with AI.

Professor Phil Tetlock's landmark research on expert forecasts revealed that the best weren't necessarily the smartest or most experienced, but those most willing to question their assumptions and update their beliefs.[125] These "superforecasters" demonstrated what he called "active open-mindedness"—a willingness to treat their own beliefs as hypotheses to be tested rather than truths to be defended. Openness to experience consistently emerges as one of the strongest predictors of creative success.

Kahneman and Tversky's research on cognitive biases illuminates why openness is so challenging.[126] Their work shows how our minds naturally resist uncertainty, seeking premature closure and false certainty. The smarter someone is, the better they often are at defending their existing beliefs. Intelligence without openness can actually entrench errors rather than correct them.[127] This helps explain why some brilliant people can be remarkably uncreative, using their intelligence to defend against rather than explore new possibilities.

Process constraints can enhance openness. Research shows that techniques like deliberate perspective-taking exercises, forced consideration of opposite viewpoints, systematic delay of judgment, and explicit acknowledgment of uncertainty can help override our natural tendency to rush to judgment.[128] Studies of creative teams show that processes that deliberately separate idea generation from evaluation help maintain the openness needed for creativity.[129]

AI interactions expose the psychological barriers to openness. Resistance to AI often arises from psychological threats to identity and expertise rather than rational evaluation. Just as medieval scholars rejected the printing press as inferior to hand-copied manuscripts, many modern experts reject AI capabilities through what psychology calls "motivated reasoning," using intelligence to defend against threatening new possibilities rather than explore them.[130]

The contrast between human and AI openness is revealing. AI systems, lacking ego investment and emotional attachments, maintain consistent receptivity to possibilities within their training. They don't suffer from confirmation bias or the need to defend existing beliefs. However, they also apparently lack the emotional and intuitive aspects of human openness that can guide creative exploration. Human-AI creative collaboration works best when humans can maintain the kind of openness that matches AI's natural receptivity.

Recent research in neuroscience helps explain why maintaining openness is so challenging. Brain imaging studies show that uncertainty and ambiguity activate the same neural circuits as physical threat, triggering defensive responses that shut down exploratory thinking.[131] This makes evolutionary sense. In dangerous environments, rapid closure on decisions often mattered more than perfect accuracy. But in modern creative contexts, these same neural circuits can prematurely shut down the very openness needed for innovation.

Educational systems might compound this challenge. Traditional education frequently rewards quick, certain answers over thoughtful exploration of possibilities. Research shows that students often learn to suppress their natural curiosity in favor of finding "correct" answers, developing a "fixed mindset" that inhibits creative openness.[132]

The key is designing processes that work with rather than against our psychological tendencies. Studies of creative practice show that specific constraints, like designated time for exploratory thinking, structured protocols for withholding judgment, and explicit permission to be wrong, can actually enhance openness by creating safe spaces for uncertainty and ambiguity.[133]

If AI is creative and we're not open to it, then we are using it as an echo chamber rather than a creative collaborator. That might be the right move, depending on the task, but it's a choice we should be conscious of.

Intuitive Judgment: The Creative Filter

At first glance, judgment might seem to oppose creativity. After all, premature judgment can kill creative possibilities.[134] That may be what is happening in my brain when I try to get an idea documented quickly.

Research shows that effective creativity relies on a nuanced form of judgment, distinct from critical thinking or evaluation. This intuitive judgment involves recognizing promising creative directions without relying solely on explicit criteria.[135]

Studies of expert performance across fields show that intuitive judgment emerges from extensive experience with *both* successes and failures.[136] But unlike routine expertise, creative judgment isn't just about pattern recognition. Research by Gary Klein and others on expert decision-making shows that creative experts develop what he calls "perceptual discrimination," which is the ability to notice subtle distinctions and possibilities that others miss.[137]

This type of judgment operates differently from analytical evaluation. Brain imaging studies show that effective creative judgment engages both deliberative and intuitive neural networks.[138] When jazz musicians improvise or writers compose, they maintain what researchers call "focused diffusion," a state that combines loose associative thinking with subtle guidance.[139] Judging too early stifles creativity; judging too late breeds chaos.

The relationship between judgment and constraints is quite nuanced. Studies of creative processes show that judgment works best when:[140]

- Initial constraints are clear but flexible
- Early judgment focuses on possibilities rather than limitations
- Evaluation criteria evolve as the creative work develops
- Final judgment considers both original intentions and emergent possibilities

Studies show that fear of judgment often inhibits creativity more than judgment itself. This has led to techniques like "yes, and ..." in improvisation, where initial judgment is deliberately suspended to allow possibilities to develop.[141]

The contrast between human and AI judgment capabilities is huge. While AI systems can process more possibilities than humans and apply consistent evaluation criteria, they currently lack the nuanced contextual judgment that humans develop through lived experience. AI might excel at spotting patterns in data, but humans better recognize which patterns matter in context. This complementarity explains why human-AI creative collaboration often works best when combining AI's processing power with human intuitive judgment.

The educational implications are significant. Traditional education often emphasizes external judgment over developing internal judgment capabilities. Research shows that students frequently learn to rely on authority figures' evaluations rather than developing their own judgment skills.[142] This may partially explain why many people struggle with creative tasks. They haven't developed the internal judgment capabilities needed to guide creative exploration.

Modern creativity training programs increasingly recognize the need to develop judgment capabilities alongside generative skills. Techniques like structured feedback protocols, iterative design processes, peer critique methods, and reflection practices help develop judgment while maintaining the openness needed for creativity.[143]

***

The relationship between humans and machines is entering uncharted territory. Our traditional understanding of machines as precise executors of human instructions has shaped how people view creativity. Machines could help refine ideas, catch errors, even extend capabilities, but the creative spark always came from humans. Humans were the generalists, the big picture thinkers, while machines were specialists. Modern GenAI significantly shifts this dynamic by enabling creative possibilities at an unprecedented scale.

AI creativity, as with other attributes, is typically compared to the best of humanity. But if you're hiring someone, you're not hiring from the best of humanity. Your comparison is AI versus the talent pool. In that comparison humanity isn't the top dog. AI's ability to generate ideas at volume, using tons of knowledge and perspectives, will be difficult for humans to ever match.

That doesn't mean we're cut out of the creative process. Instead of mere tools, AI functions as a brilliant but naive collaborator—overflowing with ideas but needing guidance. They excel at generating possibilities and drawing connections across vast knowledge networks, while humans excel at judgment, context, and understanding what matters. It's like a brilliant intern who has read everything but lacks real-world experience. They might generate amazing ideas but need human wisdom to judge which ones are actually valuable. Even a hypothetical superintelligent AI would need human wisdom to guide its capabilities toward meaningful ends.

The problem with dismissing AI as stochastic parrots was best countered by my former colleague Dr. Robert Seater, who also came up with the intern analog. "A stochastic parrot is a valuable tool for creativity." Even if AI isn't truly creative in some philosophical sense, its ability to generate novel and meaningful possibilities transforms how creative work happens.

This shift demands rethinking not just about how to use AI, but how to develop human creative capabilities. Simply waiting for copyright law or other regulations to shield creative work from AI's impact isn't a strategy. There's no guarantee the courts will agree with the artists, plus there are already strong performing examples of GenAI that use only open-source material[144] or mainly simulated data.[145]

The focus must be on developing the uniquely human aspects of creativity, especially the capacity for judgment and contextual understanding, and to minimize our drawbacks, like in openness.

The beauty of concept stretching, introduced in the last chapter, is how it naturally develops multiple creativity ingredients. As students explore concepts across contexts, they build both the scale of their knowledge network and their capacity for variation. Working with multiple examples and analogies develops comfort with volume, seeing many possibilities rather than single answers. Exploring how concepts manifest differently across contexts builds openness to new possibilities. And comparing different applications helps develop intuitive judgment about when and how concepts apply.

The ingredients of creativity explored here—scale, volume, variation, openness, and intuitive judgment—take on new significance considering AI. AI might exceed humans in some of these dimensions, but human wisdom remains essential in orchestrating AI systems toward meaningful creativity. The human role is transformed, focusing more on wisdom and judgment than raw generative power. Our prime difficulty is how to preserve the importance and beauty of purely human creations while using AI's creative boost to spark paths, such as in medicine, that should care less where the idea originated.

KEY META-PRINCIPLES

- **Ingredients for Creativity**: Exploring how scale, volume, variety, openness, and intuitive judgment influence creative outcomes, both with and without AI.

- **Open-Mindedness**: Training students to challenge assumptions, embrace diverse perspectives, and expand their creative potential by developing genuine open-mindedness.

- **Recognizing, Managing, and Refining Creative Processes**: Identifying situations that demand creativity, allocating tasks effectively between humans and AI, and understanding how processes like applying constraints or brainstorming techniques shape creative outcomes.

EXAMPLE LEARNING PROGRESSION

K-5	• Experiment with how changes in scale or variety affect creative results (e.g., drawing with different numbers of crayons). • Play games to practice open-minded thinking. • Work within constraints (e.g., creating art using only specific shapes or materials).
6-8	• Explore all five creative ingredients in hands-on projects. • Practice open-mindedness by brainstorming and sharing divergent solutions to problems. • Use constraints intentionally to guide creative processes.
9-12	• Design complex projects that integrate multiple creative ingredients. • Engage in debates or problem-solving tasks that require open-mindedness and intuitive judgment. • Experiment with constraints and analyze their effect on outcomes.
College	• Conduct in-depth experiments with the creative ingredients. • Use interdisciplinary approaches to identify creative opportunities and manage processes that balance constraints with innovation. • Explore advanced task allocation strategies between humans and AI in creative workflows.

PART II. META-LEARNING AND TEACHING

N ow that you've gotten a sense for what AI is, it's time to talk about the part that all the major media skip over, saying only that it happens.

AI neural networks are taught. The methods used to teach them are called machine learning. While it may seem that the details of how AI was developed are mere curiosities to the average person, this is a misconception. AI doesn't stop learning when the AI company finishes training it. You teach it every time you use it. Wouldn't it be great to know how it learns?

The technologist building it doesn't have to be an expert in whatever domain they're developing the AI for. They just have to set up the right environment for the AI to learn. That's not even close to how we've traditionally thought of computers and software.

In this part, I'll describe how AI has moved beyond simple if-then rules to become a true learning system, one that develops capabilities through trial, error, and continuous adaptation.

The implications are profound. When you're programming a computer, you know exactly what it will do—follow your instructions, step by step. But when you're training an AI, you're more like a teacher setting up conditions for learning. You can't directly program what you want; instead, you must figure out how to measure success, balance exploration with exploitation, and provide the right examples for concept formation.

This creates fascinating challenges. How do you define "best" when goals conflict or evolve? How do you balance allowing AI to explore new possibilities with leveraging what it already knows? How do you help it form robust concepts rather than overreacting to every situation? Perhaps most importantly, how do you understand and manage the different types of errors that emerge during learning?

These aren't just theoretical questions. As AI becomes more prevalent in our lives, understanding how it learns—and how that learning can go right or wrong—becomes increasingly crucial for everyone. There are also significant overlaps that are relevant to personal and organizational learning.

In the chapters ahead, I'll explore the machinery of AI learning, the role of adaptive learning, and how concepts emerge from examples. I'll describe why certain types of errors occur and, more importantly, what we can do about them.

The goal isn't to turn you into an AI engineer that grows AI from scratch using complex math and software packages. However, when you use AI, you are an AI product developer too. Understanding how AI learns isn't optional. It's essential.

What does it really mean for a machine to learn?

6.

LEARNING

M achine learning has two core forms that parallel familiar educational approaches. This chapter explores how neural networks learn through *optimization*, a process where an AI neural network searches for the best possible solution by adjusting its internal connection weights to improve performance. "Best" can be defined by minimizing errors, maximizing some benefit, or balancing multiple objectives.

Optimization is most effective in stable, well-defined problems with consistent goals and clear success metrics. This aligns with behaviorist pedagogy, rooted in B.F. Skinner's work,[146] that views learning as a process of conditioning shaped through structured feedback, and where the goals and tactics are not adaptable by the student.

The next chapter explores AI's parallel to constructivist pedagogy, where learning happens through experience and adaptation, with evolving goals and conditions.

I already introduced you to one optimization challenge in the Prologue. Litsa was trying to maximize the output firing of a frog neuron by choosing which combination of pixels might elicit the top output.

A common example of optimization is factory efficiency. Success metrics may balance multiple objectives—low costs, high output, and good working conditions. The core task is to define "best" with measurable criteria and systematically refine operations to achieve it.

We encounter optimization problems every day. What's the best route to work? The best schedule for this week? Maybe you've streamlined a boring task by gradually improving its efficiency. In each case, you are trying to search for the best solution given many options.

Optimization is necessary and possible when:

- Many possible solutions exist
- The objective is well-defined, measurable, stable, and directly influenced by choices
- Each learning choice is independent

ChatGPT's main neural network learns through optimization, predicting the next text output. The environment (training data) remains fixed, and the goal (minimizing prediction error) is measurable. While each output is independently generated, it depends on prior text. That's handled by feeding past AI output back into the network as an input.

I'll start the optimization discussion a bit strangely.

OPTI-BOT

Imagine you are exploring another earth-size planet, but you're in orbit and a robot I'll call Opti-Bot is at the surface. You control the robot's position.

Opti-Bot has some peculiar features. For one, it can't move across the ground, but in this Star Trek fantasy world that doesn't stop it from being able to teleport precisely to any location on the planet.

Each time you choose a location, Opti-Bot reports its ground-level altitude.

Your task is to reliably find the highest point on the planet in a reasonable amount of time using only Opti-Bot.

There are constraints. The robot can power a limited number of teleportations, and each move and altitude measurement take time. Oh, and Opti-Bot is blind. It has no camera, or any other sensors beyond the altitude-measuring instrument.

Sure, there are gaps in this analogy—what, NASA couldn't afford a camera? The people who built the orbiter hadn't heard of RADAR? Then there's the paradox that Opti-Bot can't know what spot to teleport to unless it knows the ground level. It'll teleport into solid rock or gassy nothingness.

Hey ... whatever. It's an analogy. You get to hop around, you get the altitude everywhere you hop, you can't sense anything else, and you have to find the highest peak.

How would you go about this task?

You might teleport to every degree of latitude and longitude—360 × 360 = 129,600 locations (assuming an Earth-sized planet). At the equator, that's roughly 69 miles between each point.

But we know some mountains can be very steep, and it's unclear what terrain this new planet has. A gap of 69 miles is too big; we'd risk skipping over the tallest peak. At a tenth of a degree, that jumps to 13 million locations! If it takes a minute to get the altitude at each location, decide where to go next, then teleport, then it would take almost 25 years to complete.

This strategy, known as exhaustive search, quickly becomes impractical. There are just too many possibilities.

Let's try another approach. What if you compare the altitudes of two or more nearby locations, and take short teleports to continue in the direction of higher altitude? If that's done until no other direction is uphill, then it's a peak.

That might get you to a pretty high altitude if you are lucky enough to start somewhere in a major mountain range, but this "hill climbing" strategy gets you to a peak. It doesn't get you to the highest peak. Maybe it only gets you to the top of the mulch pile in our alien counterpart's back yard.

A better approach might sample the altitudes at some random locations and then hill climb from the ones that are already at significant altitudes. That doesn't guarantee the highest peak either, but at least you'd be likely to end up in the Himalayas somewhere, even if not Mt. Everest.

There's no perfect way to do this. The optimal strategy is too dependent on the nature of the underlying terrain. A planet as smooth as a cue ball might have a top altitude of a few meters, reachable by hill climbing from any location on the planet. Or it could have Grand Canyons and Mt. Everest's all over the place.

Beyond illustrating optimization challenges, the Opti-Bot metaphor foreshadows key AI learning principles. The same fundamental trade-offs between thorough search, quick improvement, and exploring multiple starting points shape how AI— or any other higher intelligence—figures out what's best when presented with lots of options.

UNDERSTANDING OPTIMIZATION

An AI trainer guides the system to find the best solution based on a defined metric. The internals of the AI are changed to find a strong solution according to the metric assigned for best.

That trainer is choosing and customizing a method for exploring an incredibly complex terrain. They are not metaphorically in the orbiter directing the robot. Rather, they are suppling the strategy for the planet search.

In my planetary example there are two traveling dimensions, the inputs: latitude and longitude. The third dimension, altitude, is the measurement of best, the output. An AI processing an image has as many dimensions as the number of pixels, each defined by intensity and color. Machine learning methods are searching for peaks in sometimes millions or billions of imaginary dimensions, without knowing much about what the actual terrain looks like.

Exhaustive search, hill climbing, and random sampling echo how we tackle complex problems in life. Sometimes we need to be thorough, checking every possibility before making an important decision. Other times we need to quickly improve from where we are, seeking fast and better over slow and best. And sometimes we need to try multiple starting points, knowing that where we begin affects where we end up. Understanding these trade-offs can help students think more systematically about any kind of improvement process, whether developing a skill, solving a problem, or working with AI to find solutions.

If the terrain is complex, you aren't likely to find the planet's highest peak in any reasonable time frame. AI likely won't either in its oodles bigger search space. AI is error prone, as are our brains, in part because the optimization challenge is really hard.

AI often learns well enough, but perfection is rarely feasible for complex challenges. In many challenges, good enough is OK, better than spending forever getting to perfect. "Perfect is the enemy of good," goes the adage. In AI training, the nature of the enemy is the computing power, energy cost, and time to train.

Students will face increasingly complex optimization challenges in their futures. They'll need to balance multiple competing factors in their decisions, from career choices to resource allocation to environmental impact. They'll need to recognize when perfect solutions aren't possible or worth the cost, and when good enough is truly adequate. They'll need to understand why different approaches work better for different types of problems. Why sometimes it's better to thoroughly analyze all options, and other times better to quickly adapt and improve.

Perhaps most importantly, they'll need to recognize optimization problems when they see them, whether they appear in personal decisions, professional challenges, or societal issues. That's partly because AI is important in helping people solve optimization problems (addressed in Volume 2), so the principles go beyond training AI. In addition, thinking about improvement and trade-offs is becoming as fundamental as reading in our increasingly complex world.

In both AI and human learning, improvement isn't accidental. It requires a systematic way to adjust behavior based on a learning experience. In AI systems, this process is explicit and programmed. In humans, it happens through complex biological and psychological mechanisms. But in both cases, effective learning requires similar elements:

- a system that can change (design)
- a process for making those changes (learning mechanism)
- a strategy for guiding changes (pedagogy)
- a way to measure success (assessment)

Understanding how AI implements these elements sheds light on learning systems in general.

I've already discussed deep neural networks (the design), which can analyze a huge range of patterns. Now I'll get into AI's learning mechanism, pedagogies, and assessments.

THE LEARNING MECHANISM

Training an AI neural network involves adjusting neuron connection strengths. Manually tweaking weights isn't practical for complex tasks. Machine learning's purpose is to let the system learn on its own.

The learning mechanism isn't directly adjustable in human brains. Teachers can't manually adjust neural connections, but AI engineers design and refine the "brain."

An AI trainer has a similar role to controlling Opti-Bot's mapping of another planet. They (or training software, really) know where the robot has been and the altitude at each of those spots. AI trainers calculate how well the AI did at each training step. They use some other suitable metric instead of altitude, and the neural net weight settings instead of latitude and longitude for each of those metric measurements.

Deep learning, a family of techniques, made deep neural networks effective learners. The challenge was figuring out how to teach all the layers, especially the early ones. Deep learning addressed this by enabling feedback at every network layer, allowing gradual improvement in pattern recognition. This ability to effectively train large, multi-layered neural networks, combined with massive amounts of data and computing power, is what enables modern AI to tackle complex tasks that were once thought impossible for machines.

For many readers, this level of understanding of AI's learning mechanism is sufficient. How the neural network weights are adjusted doesn't matter much to those who aren't pursuing a computer science career.

Those interested in a deeper look at how these principles were discovered and implemented can continue reading. Others may wish to skip the next section, continuing with "AI Pedagogies."

Don't skip that one though. Each interaction with GenAI is a teaching process. Some of the principles of pedagogy, of putting an AI in position to learn, are very useful in AI prompting, and relate to human teaching paradigms.

THE EVOLUTION OF DEEP LEARNING (OPTIONAL)

Deep neural networks had a major obstacle to widespread use in the 1990s and much of the 2000s. They were really hard to train. It required the invention of deep learning, pioneered again by Geoff Hinton.

The trainers know one more thing I didn't mention yet. They know the AI is a layered neural net, and the last layer of the network is responsible for the AI output.

Logically, adjusting the last layer's connections first makes sense—it directly impacts the output. Changing something in the first layer of the network has a much more indirect influence.

Also, by looking at the "best" metric in the local vicinity of each iteration of network connection settings, basically looking at the slope of the ground, the learning algorithm can know which way is uphill.

Before deep learning, neural networks were typically trained using backpropagation, which adjusts layers from last to first, guiding neurons "uphill" in weight changes. Hinton was an author on that paper too, in 1986.[147]

The problem is that if there are a lot of layers then it takes a long time to get the early layers to learn. It's like the champagne glass pyramid at a wedding. The glass at the top fills fast, but it takes a lot of time and champagne to fill the bottom tier. From the point of view of one of the bottom glasses, a big change from the bottle pour evokes only a small effect locally.

This is referred to as the *vanishing gradient* problem, with gradient in the Opti-Bot example meaning the slope of the ground at an altitude measurement point. At the final layer of the network, the slope is obvious, but for any neuron in the early layers of the neural net, it's hard to tell which way is uphill.

In 2006, Geoff Hinton was lead author on a paper that dealt with the vanishing gradient problem. [148] His solution was to preset the network weights to get it in the vicinity of the right answer and then use backpropagation. The approach starts at the first layers of the network and makes sure that each layer, when information at that layer is combined, can be used to reconstruct the input data accurately. Then backpropagation is applied in the second step. It basically tries to make sure the network is preserving the information in the input data. This doesn't guarantee the network is near the biggest mountain range, but it at least ignores all the crappy lowlands.

Hinton's approach paid off. In 2012 they blew away their peers in an image analysis competition using deep neural nets and deep learning.[149] That competition, and Hinton's team contribution, was one of the seminal moments in AI history.

There are now many variations of both the deep neural net architecture and the deep learning process. Engineers don't use

Hinton's 2006 approach anymore. They've learned other tricks that help better.[150]

One addition to backpropagation is usually some form of randomness added to the hill climbing process, to help avoid the learning process getting stuck on top of a small mole hill.

One improvement involves randomly ignoring, or "dropping out," a set of neurons at each training step.[151] Some methods also prune the network periodically, permanently removing weak connections.[152] This forces the network to generalize better and learn more robust patterns. Finally, advanced optimization methods adjust the learning rate dynamically during training, which improves both the pace of learning and the ultimate performance.[153]

Some innovations in the neural network architecture made it easier for deep learning. For example, in the mid-10s researchers started adding some connections between neurons that skip levels, to further help the vanishing gradient problem.[154] This finally allowed truly deep networks of hundreds of layers to be trained effectively.

My metaphor for this is a do-it-yourself ice dam prevention method for roofs. I learned this during a year of record snowpack in the Boston area. You fill nylons with salt, and then place them perpendicular to the roof edge, hanging a bit over. This creates channels for water to drain instead of refreezing. Similarly, skip connections in the neural net can help prevent neural net learning "ice dams."

Neuroscientists had known about such hierarchy-skipping connections in the brain for a long time, but it seems the AI approach wasn't brain motivated. The discovery of skip connections' effectiveness in artificial neural networks did generate interest among neuroscientists to study similar patterns in biological neural networks more closely.

Deep neural nets and deep learning rely on a ton of examples of the data needed for a decision, along with the right answer, but by the 2000s it was no longer practically impossible to get the data and train a deep neural net. (I'll get into training data and its influence in Chapter 8). Computing and data availability had finally caught up. AI came out of its so-called "winter" where promises of better AI were stalled by tech limitations. The availability of large, human-labeled data sets became AI gold. Deep learning woke AI research and development out of a slumber. AI developers had a general purpose "chip", to use a hardware analogy, that can be applied to a huge range of applications. Even as AI has evolved from specialized to general purpose AI models, deep neural nets trained with deep learning are still the main paradigms.

Geoffrey Hinton is often referred to as one of the "godfathers" of modern AI. He went on to work at Google Research for many years, continuing to make his mark on AI advancements. He retired shortly after ChatGPT's emergence. He is now a strong voice of concern about major, even existential, AI risks.[155]

AI PEDAGOGIES

Just as students learn differently depending on how they're taught, AI systems learn through distinct approaches. Understanding those methods directly affects how we interact with AI systems and what they can learn from us. When you prompt an AI, you're essentially choosing a teaching method, whether you realize it or not. If good teaching means placing a learning engine in the right conditions, what are those conditions?

As with teaching students, there are several pedagogical options. AI can be told precisely what to do, given general instructions, given a task but no instructions, or left to figure things out on its own, including what to do.

Supervised learning provides example problems and correct answers but without teaching a process for solving them. It's often the preferred choice for AI training. The AI is trained with application-specific data examples and the correct solution (the label) for each example. Just as a teacher would mark a student's assignment based on how closely their answers match the correct ones, supervised learning's "best" measurement compares AI's answers with the correct answer (often, but not always, provided by humans).

For example, when an AI learns to recognize objects in images, it's shown millions of labeled images ("this is a cat", "this is a dog") and learns to recognize patterns that distinguish between them. The same principle applies to language models like ChatGPT, which learn by predicting what words should come next in vast amounts of text.

An error minimization objective is super common and is most often associated with supervised learning. (Minimizing error is learning to find the lowest valley in the terrain rather than the highest peak.) Error minimization metrics have broad applicability. It takes advantage of human expertise without having to pre-guess what aspect of that expertise should be learned.

AI language models have multiple AI components, but for most the core is a deep neural network trained via supervised learning. The task posed to the network during its training is to minimize the statistical error between tokens (a character sequence) that the AI puts out and the token that was actually next in the text example. The input data itself supplies the correct answer, so this kind of scheme is called *self-supervised learning*.

Supervised learning thrives on diverse, clearly labeled examples. If you're giving AI a set of examples, then give it the right kinds of examples according to the transformation purpose, as covered in Chapter 2, but also give it your interpretation of the example. Was it chosen to illustrate something specific? The interpretations serve as training labels, helping the AI understand the specific boundaries between your categories, or the range extent of a regression measure.

Sometimes though, the correct answers are either unavailable or unknown. If you're using AI to help analyze the chemicals in a sample of water, let's say, then you may have no clue about the range of possibilities. That's fine if you're looking for something specific, but if you're trying to discover what's in the water then you don't want to assume the answers.

That's the time for *unsupervised learning*. The AI is simply given the data and tasked with finding patterns within it. It doesn't get a right answer, or any answer at all, as part of training. Unsupervised learning tries to see similarity without assuming meaning or labels ahead of time.

A teacher might give students a pile of objects and ask them to categorize them freely, without guidance. Then subsequent discussion could then be about whether the groupings seem logical, without providing an exact "right" or "wrong" answer.

Unsupervised learning is particularly powerful when exploring new territories. For instance, AI models that analyze social media patterns or customer behaviors often use unsupervised learning to discover natural groupings and trends that humans might not have thought to look for.

When exploring creative possibilities with AI, you can apply unsupervised learning principles by giving it freedom to find patterns without rigid constraints. Instead of asking "Write a story about courage," you might prompt "Explore different ways courage can manifest in unexpected situations." This allows the AI to draw upon broader pattern associations from its training.

There are various forms of unsupervised learning schemes, many of which don't use neural nets. Clustering methods try to find training example sub-groups that are most similar statistically. Imagine you've asked for feedback on some aspect of your school or classroom, and you want to know the most prevalent subgroups in the responses. A clustering method could be useful in telling you the aspects of feedback that matter most, potentially disrupting a biased expectation.

It's useful to have scatter plots like the ones in Part I in mind. The examples for many challenges will show higher density of data examples in some regions than others; those are the clusters. Since clumps can exist at different scales, often the trainer will have to give the learning method a clue about how many clusters to expect. Clustering applies a group label to something based on similarity to a prototype. The labeled is applied to the group after training the AI, not while training. A dog that truly looks like a cat will probably end up with the wrong label when clustered. One common method (K-nearest neighbors) clusters based on analysis of patterns in the statistical "distance" between data examples in the scatter plot space.

In *semi-supervised learning*, the AI is given a small amount of labeled data (with correct answers) and a larger amount of unlabeled data (without answers), and it learns from both. This is like a teacher giving students a few examples with clear solutions and then providing a much larger set of incomplete problems for the students to figure out. The key is that the AI uses what it learned from the labeled data to make sense of the unlabeled data.

Google DeepMind's AlphaFold, which predicts protein structures, exemplifies semi-supervised learning.[156] Its developers won the 2024 Nobel Prize in Chemistry.[157] There is a limited amount of labeled data in the form of known protein structures. Most protein sequences have unknown structures. *AlphaFold* uses a combination of labeled data (known structures) and unlabeled data (unknown structures) to make predictions. The labeled data helps guide the model, but it must generalize this learning to predict the structures for the large set of unlabeled protein sequences. This allows the system to build highly accurate models for proteins where no direct experimental data is available.

Imagine giving an AI a mix of student essays, where only a few have grades and feedback while the majority do not. Instead of explicitly teaching the AI the grading criteria upfront, you ask it to analyze both the graded and ungraded essays to infer a grading rubric. The AI must first learn from the small set of graded work, then use that understanding to assess and develop a rubric for the rest.

This approach can be preferable to simply providing the graded essays because it allows the AI to recognize broader patterns in the student work, rather than just mimicking the grading of a limited sample. By incorporating the full dataset, the AI may create a rubric that better captures variations in writing quality, leading to more consistent and adaptable grading.

When interacting with modern AI systems, you're often engaging with these different learning approaches simultaneously. For example, when asking an AI to help grade assignments, you might

- Show it examples of graded work (supervised learning)
- Let it find patterns in ungraded assignments (unsupervised learning)

- Provide a few key examples while letting it analyze many more unlabeled ones (semi-supervised learning)
- Have it learn from its evaluation of its own attempts to reconstruct assignment content (self-supervised learning)

You should be applying a pedagogy when you prompt AI. You're "transferring in" the language model and building on top of it, in an analogous way to the extra knowledge teachers add to students' minds.

AI'S ASSESSMENT

For AI to learn, it needs clear signals about what constitutes improvement. The assessment—captured in the "best" metric—is the key feedback that helps guide learning. Without it, the AI would be blind, unable to know if it was getting better or worse. This measurement challenge shapes both how AI develops capabilities and why it sometimes learns unexpected or undesired behaviors.

AI only learns when given the right feedback. Otherwise, it learns—but not necessarily what you intended.

Supervised learning—where answers accompany practice problems—optimizes for minimal error between AI predictions and correct responses. There are a few different forms of the error calculation that, for example, weight outlier examples differently, but error minimization is an extremely common choice. A form of minimum error metric is used to teach many GenAI models.

Minimizing error lets AI developers avoid pre-selecting which input features matter most. The data examples and correct answers define what to learn.

Unsupervised learning is inherently about defining best as some statistical aspect of the data, with the AI learning to minimize or maximize that property. Again, the goal of the learning is abstract and not directly related to human goals and values.

Many assume AI engineers explicitly shape or overlook the goals, values, and biases in trained models. They don't direct the AI like you do when talking to a language model. The choices are in the selection of the data examples and the nature of the "correct" answer. The impact of those choices can't be understood until the AI is trained and tested. Increasingly the traditional metrics of GenAI assessment are limiting, assessing only aspects of capability in incomplete ways, not unlike standardized tests in education.

When prompting AI, minimizing errors requires defining what type of errors matter and clarifying the problem. A teacher's assessments significantly influence what students perceive as important. AI follows similar learning breadcrumbs. The error signal is the feedback that tells the system how well it's doing. If we don't choose the right signal, the AI might focus on improving in ways that don't solve the real problem we care about. Deciding on what to measure and how to measure it is crucial.

AI can sometimes learn the wrong thing if developers are not careful. One AI model designed to detect cancerous moles from images instead picked up on surgical scars unrelated to skin health.[158] In teaching AI how to play the game CoastRunners, OpenAI developers forgot to include completing the game course as an objective, resulting in an AI that kept repeatedly gathering a mid-course reward instead of finishing.[159]

AI identifies patterns, but they may not align with consumer needs. This happens when the training data doesn't teach the lessons engineers wish or AI designs favor company interests over consumer needs.

Sometimes, measurements are stand-ins—or proxies—for what we really want. That can lead to unexpected and undesired behavior. Imagine a school that wants to encourage reading, so it starts rewarding students based on the number of books they check out from the library. Students quickly catch on and begin checking out lots of books without actually reading them, just to get the rewards. In this case, the number of books checked out is a proxy for reading, but it doesn't ensure that students are actually reading or learning from the books. Proxy measurements can have unintended downsides, though they are often predictable.

A real-world example of a damaging proxy measurement is how social media sites optimize for user engagement. Companies aim to keep people on their sites longer because it's presumed to lead to higher revenue and market control. To do this, they design algorithms that show content likely to grab attention and encourage interaction, emphasizing sensational news or emotionally charged posts. While this increases engagement, it can also spread misinformation, create echo chambers, or heighten divisions among users. By optimizing solely for engagement, these platforms promote content that's harmful or misleading.

AI optimization training usually focuses on optimizing a single number. Having one clear goal makes it easier for the AI to learn and improve. If we try to optimize multiple things at once—like accuracy, speed, and resource usage—the AI might get "confused" because improving one area could make another worse. Plus, as soon as there are multiple metrics then the relative importance of each metric must be set. By combining different objectives into one overall metric, we provide a clear direction for the AI's learning process. It's similar to giving a student an overall grade that combines homework, tests, and participation, so they understand their standing in the class with a single, comprehensive score.

This is also akin to corporate decision-making processes where multiple solution attributes—like cost, quality, and implementation time—are evaluated. Teams might assign weights to each attribute based on their importance and calculate a total score for each solution option. By converting multiple criteria into a single composite score, organizations can make decisions more straightforwardly. A straightforward process does not mean it will be an accurate, reasonable, or unbiased judgment though.

Understanding how AI optimizes for measurement signals can help us craft better prompts. Instead of asking an AI to "make this text better," which leaves the optimization target unclear, specify what "better" means: "Revise this text to improve clarity by using shorter sentences and simpler vocabulary while maintaining all key information." This gives the AI clear criteria to optimize against.

There are methods for AI training that allow for optimization of multiple metrics. The methods rely on the notion that when there are multiple objectives there are probably multiple valid combinations of those metrics. Grading a student essay could acknowledge that an essay strong in evidence but weaker in clarity isn't strictly better or worse than one with opposite strengths. A factory optimization could acknowledge that low cost and high quality both matter, but there are different valid settings depending on whether serving an upscale or down-market consumer.

This is called Pareto optimization. While it's an appealing concept for AI training, in practice it's still a technical challenge. It's often simpler to use the other main AI learning approach suited for changing, situation-dependent behaviors. Assessment challenges grow even more complex in dynamic environments. Such situations are addressed in the next chapter.

***

Understanding the process of learning is incredibly important for educators and anyone interacting with AI. Just as teachers shape how students learn, we also influence how AI systems learn and behave. When we interact with AI, we're essentially teaching it. Knowing how learning works helps us ensure that AI systems develop in ways that are beneficial and align with our values.

The principles of learning—like how we measure progress, the methods we use to teach, and the ways we adjust our approach—apply to both human education and AI development.

So let me ask an uncomfortable question. If learning requires clear measurement of what we value, processes for change, and appropriate forms of guidance, how well do current education systems embody these principles?

Consider the fundamental disconnect in education. Everyone says they value durable skills like critical thinking, creativity, and adaptability, yet the measurements the system drives toward are more testable content knowledge. This is like training an AI system to optimize for proxy metrics we know don't capture what really matters. The assessment feedback signal is wrong.

Even with better measurements, education systems face structural barriers. Standards, infrastructure, scheduling, and institutional inertia create a rigid framework resistant to change. It's as if we've built a learning system with frozen neural connections, technically capable of change, but practically unable to adapt. The system doesn't have a good learning mechanism.

The education system's learning approach has flaws too. Education largely follows a supervised learning paradigm, where "correct" answers are predefined through standards and testing. There's limited room for unsupervised learning—discovering what naturally works well—or learning from real-world outcomes. The system is perhaps best described as self-supervised, learning primarily from its own historical patterns rather than external feedback. Like an AI trained only on its own outputs, this creates a closed loop that can perpetuate existing limitations rather than evolve to meet changing needs. *Model collapse*, the demise predicted by some for AI models when they are trained on their own output, might apply to education more.[160]

As AI reshapes society, education must become a learning system itself—measuring what matters, adapting strategies, and balancing learning approaches. Understanding how AI learns might help us recognize what's missing in institutional learning processes.

Optimization problems are everywhere. The principles of establishing a target and trying to change a set of factors that will get a population (of neurons, people, organizations, or AI) closer to the target is a ubiquitous teaching challenge. Learning more about learning empowers educators and students and helps in teaching AI via prompting.

KEY META-PRINCIPLES

- **The Iterative Nature of Improvement**: Many learning challenges are optimization problems, where success depends on setting clear objectives, systematically testing adjustments, and refining strategies based on measurable progress.

- **AI Pedagogies**: Different AI teaching strategies are used for different aims and constraints.

- **Assessment**: Learning requires clear and actionable feedback mechanisms.

EXAMPLE LEARNING PROGRESSION

K-5	• Identify how feedback helps improve performance in everyday tasks. • Explore simple examples of goal setting and iterative improvement. • Recognize that different challenges may need different strategies, and that improvement happens through trial and adjustment.
6-8	• Analyze how feedback influences improvement in personal or group activities, emphasizing step-by-step refinement toward a goal. • Discuss why different AI learning methods are suited to different goals. • Explore optimization by experimenting with incremental adjustments, testing, and refinement in hands-on projects.
9-12	• Investigate real-world applications of AI learning methods. • Apply principles of optimization and learning pedagogy to GenAI use. • Develop or work with simple AI models to teach specific tasks or solve defined problems.
College	• Design strategies to fine-tune AI models or improve their performance through iterative adjustments. • Experiment with multi-method approaches to optimize AI performance for real-world tasks. • Critically assess how feedback and constraints affect learning outcomes in advanced AI systems compared to human learning processes.

7.

ADAPTIVE

A ll of this sounds so oversimplified. It's time I turn up the difficulty knob.

In the previous chapter, I talked about how AI learns in static environments where goals and conditions remain fixed. But just as teachers must adapt to changing classroom dynamics and evolving educational needs, AI must learn to navigate shifting environments. This adaptive learning represents a fundamental shift from simple optimization to something far more complex and realistic.

I've described one form of AI learning—optimization. If you want to find the best solution to a fixed problem with many choices, you identify what "best" is in a single metric, and you keep incrementally moving toward the peak or valley.

Oh, if life were that easy.

Imagine the Opti-Bot's mission is finding areas suitable for life instead of the peak ground level. This requires measuring factors like temperature, moisture, chemical composition, and radiation levels. As the last chapter discussed, these factors can be merged into a single fitness score for optimization. But even with a carefully crafted fitness metric, this challenge differs fundamentally from simple optimization because:

- *Actions can't be redone.* Sometimes choices permanently change future options. Opti-Bot might have limited testing resources. If it uses too many before reaching promising spots, there's no way to start over.

143

- *Actions change the situation.* Conditions might shift because of prior AI decisions. Opti-Bot's presence might interfere with its own measurements by warming the area, introducing contaminants, or disrupting geological formations.
- *There are both short- and long-term goals.* Opti-Bot's long-term goal might be to find the best place for life, but its short-term goal is to avoid getting damaged.
- *There could be an adversary.* If something is actively working against Opti-Bot, like a rival bot or silicone-eating microorganisms—it needs to adapt, not just optimize.
- *The definition of success can change.* If Opti-Bot finds life in an unexpected place, it may need to reconsider which environmental factors are most important.
- *Unpredictable changes are inevitable.* Some problems change in ways that can't be predicted or controlled. A sudden dust storm could alter planetary features or Opti-Bot might have a malfunction to compensate for.

Educators are familiar with dynamic situations like this. A teacher might start with a clear plan, but things could evolve. Each concept a student masters opens different possible paths for what they could learn next. Teaching methods that worked initially might become less effective as students advance. Student interests could change based on what they learn. Early educational choices create or limit future opportunities. And the very process of learning changes how students engage with new material.

There is another form of AI learning that deals with dynamic situations. It has advanced more slowly than supervised learning, but recently the advances are accelerating. It's ultimately better matched to the changing world we make decisions in.

It's called *Reinforcement Learning (RL)*, and it has similarity to constructivist theories in human and animal learning, where iterative exploration is emphasized. Neuroscientists and behavior researchers are now examining past theories through RL lenses.[161]

With RL, learning isn't about a single best outcome but about policies, constraints, guidelines, rewards and punishment.

REINFORCEMENT LEARNING

Reinforcement learning shines in environments where objectives aren't fully clear, feedback is sparse or delayed, and decisions need to be made in complex, often adversarial conditions. In these situations, the AI must discover both the goal and the right ways to interact with its environment. The environment could be the real-world space around a robot and aspects of task context, or the text from an LLM user.

Supervised learning is a drill master enforcing what is learned, while unsupervised learning is a detective finding historical patterns. In contrast, RL is about discovery. The AI must interact with its environment, make choices, and adjust its behavior based on rewards or penalties that are often delayed or indirect.

Imagine teaching a young child to ride a bike. Even if they could read, you wouldn't give them a manual with step-by-step instructions (like conventional software) or place them in every possible scenario and grade their biking skills (as in supervised learning). And you wouldn't show them videos of people riding bikes with no other instruction (unsupervised learning). Instead, the child learns through trial and error, guided by feedback and experience. They may fall (negative feedback) or stay upright for a few seconds (positive feedback), gradually developing an intuitive sense of balance.

A simpler example might be teaching a robot to navigate through a basic maze to find a charging station. Let's assume the robot starts with no knowledge of the maze. At any point, it can move forward, turn left, or turn right. When it reaches the charging station, it gets "rewarded" with power. If it bumps into a wall, it gets "punished" with a small power loss.

Through trial and error, RL helps the robot develop policies, but not in the way humans write policies. Unlike explicit rules (e.g., 'if there's a wall ahead, turn right'), RL policies function as statistical models mapping situations to actions. The policy captures subtle patterns that might be hard to express in simple if-then rules, though it's appropriate for students to start their learning with rule-based policies.

Rather than trying to match predetermined correct answers, the maze-navigating AI must discover what works through experience. For example, the robot's policy might learn that turning right is slightly more successful than turning left in certain situations, but this preference might shift based on tiny details about the robot's position, previous movements, or sensor readings. RL policies represent these nuanced relationships mathematically.

Think of it like an experienced driver's feel for handling a car. They've developed intuitions that would be nearly impossible to write down as a set of rules, but these intuitions consistently guide their actions. RL policies are similar. They encode complex patterns of what tends to work, learned through experience.

The robot isn't just optimizing for immediate goals (like avoiding walls) but for the long-term goal of finding the charger efficiently. Sometimes it might need to take a longer path that eventually leads to success to avoid complications on a shorter path. This balancing of immediate versus long-term rewards is a key aspect of RL.

Unlike supervised learning, where an AI is given clear examples of right and wrong answers, reinforcement learning involves discovering what works through interaction with an environment. The feedback often comes after a series of decisions, making it harder to know which specific actions were good or bad. Did the robot fail to find the charger because of a wrong turn at the beginning, or one near the end?

The maze example illustrates several key aspects of reinforcement learning:

- *States and Actions:* At any moment, the robot is in a particular state (its location and what it sees around it) and must choose from available actions (move forward, turn left, turn right).
- *Rewards and Penalties:* The robot receives feedback based on its actions, like positive rewards for finding the charger, and negative penalties for hitting walls.
- *Policy Development:* Over time, the robot learns a statistical model that maps situations to actions.

Real-world applications of reinforcement learning are far more complex than this maze example, but the basic principles remain the same. A self-driving car must learn which actions (accelerate, brake, turn) work best in various situations (heavy traffic, weather conditions, different road types).

ALPHAGO

Reinforcement learning gained prominence through AI mastering games. A landmark moment was when DeepMind's *AlphaGo* beat the world's best Go player in 2016.[162] My sense is many outside of AI treated it as a publicity stunt of little true value. Those in the AI world saw how the challenges of game play relate to everyday life. They knew AI's game mastery was a big deal.

The game of Go is immensely complex, much more so than chess, with more possible configurations than there are atoms in the universe. For decades, AI researchers had struggled to teach machines to play Go at a competitive level, because traditional AI methods like supervised learning or rule-based systems were insufficient.

AlphaGo used RL to master Go by playing millions of games against itself. Each time, it received feedback based on whether it won or lost, and over time it learned which strategies maximized its chances of winning.

Go isn't won by a single great move. Success relies on sequences of actions—moves that seem poor initially may enable brilliant strategies later. This is where RL shines; it enables the AI to think not just about immediate rewards but about long-term strategies too.

Mastering complex, long-term strategies have implications well beyond gaming. In education, many important outcomes, from student engagement to conceptual understanding, depend on sequences of decisions rather than single actions. Building durable skills like critical thinking and creativity are long-term efforts, but captive to a bunch of short-term decisions.

In the early days of reinforcement learning, systems kept track of all the possible states of the environment explicitly (game board layout and history) and all the possible AI actions (possible moves). Those could be giant tables of policies when there are tons of states and actions.

AlphaGo's success wasn't just a testament to the power of AI, but specifically to the strength of RL combined with deep neural networks. As the number of possible states and actions grows, it becomes harder and harder for the AI to keep track of everything and learn the policies for what's best in any given situation. In Go, there are so many possible board configurations that storing all of them explicitly would be impossible. But by using deep neural networks, *AlphaGo* was able to generalize across different board states, recognizing patterns and learning to evaluate which moves were most likely to lead to long-term success.

The combination of RL with deep learning on neural networks—known as deep reinforcement learning (DRL)—has proven to be a powerful technique not just for games like Go, but for many real-world applications.

Lots of challenges are even harder than Go. At least with a game you know who won or lost, and you can play the game as many times as you want to learn the lessons. AI board game solvers demonstrate one aspect of the RL value, which is the ability to balance short- and long-term objectives, particularly in adversarial situations.

Harder problems include ones where the goals, policies, or the environment the AI is in may shift over time.

RL is used to teach robots how to navigate physical spaces, manipulate objects, and even collaborate with other robots or humans. In autonomous driving, RL is used to help vehicles learn how to navigate complex road environments. The vehicle needs to plan its actions in real-time, anticipating how other actors in the environment might behave and adjusting its strategy based on those predictions.

EXPLOITATION VERSUS EXPLORATION

Imagine the maze-navigating robot has found one path to the charging station. Should it keep using that same path (*exploitation*), or should it spend time searching for potentially better routes (*exploration*)?

This is the exploration-exploitation dilemma at the heart of reinforcement learning. Exploitation means taking advantage of what you already know works. Exploration means trying new things, even when you're not sure they'll work. The challenge lies in balancing these two approaches.

This balance shifts over time. Early in learning, exploration is crucial. The robot needs to try many different paths to understand the maze's layout. But as it gains experience, it should gradually shift toward exploitation, using its accumulated knowledge more often. Students also need more experimentation when learning new concepts but can rely more on proven methods as they gain mastery.

Understanding this balance can help educators, too. A purely exploitative approach like drilling students on one specific problem-solving method might produce quick results but limit their ability to handle novel situations. Conversely, a purely exploratory approach like open-ended discovery without guidance might leave students struggling to develop reliable skills.

There are lessons in AI reinforcement learning that abstractly relate to student learning. Allowing an AI agent to explore its environment without immediate feedback can lead to more robust learning outcomes. Research has showed that AI agents equipped with curiosity-driven exploration performed better in complex environments by discovering novel patterns without relying solely on external rewards.[163]

Adding negative reinforcement can sometimes hinder the learning process.[164] It may discourage exploration, causing the agent to avoid certain actions without understanding their potential long-term benefits. AI can sometimes find a clever way around negative reinforcement that is just a trick way to avoid the feedback. Negative feedback is a murkier signal because knowing something is wrong doesn't necessarily inform correct behavior. Excessive negative feedback can limit an AI's ability to discover optimal behaviors.

Behaviorist education theories, ala Skinner,[165] emphasize the exploitation aspect of learning, especially by focusing on the feedback (assessments) and using fixed, extrinsic goals. It has mostly been applied to training for precise, repeatable behaviors. Behaviorist pedagogies are often applied to problems that can be solved quickly, and the theory practically requires breaking complex problems into separate, small pieces. Problems requiring a sequence of judgment steps, or where it's difficult to define success, or when it's unclear what situations the learner will encounter, aren't as easily addressed. Behaviorist curricula aren't usually conducive to much student exploration.

Constructivist approaches emphasize exploration, critical thinking, and knowledge construction through experience and reflection, often incorporating integrative challenges.[166] However, feedback can be delayed, infrequent, and hard to interpret. The process is slow and thus variation can be sacrificed; variation is key to decisions about when concepts are useful.

While constructivist approaches emphasize exploration and personal discovery, they are most effective when paired with guidance and feedback. For example, when learning to read, students benefit from exploring texts but also need instruction on words and phonemes to build their skills efficiently. Exploration enriched by guidance accelerates learning.

I think the old debate between behaviorists and constructivists is a bit like the discussions about nature versus nurture in biology. Both educational camps are trying to leverage brain learning modes (of which reinforcement learning is only one), but neither one does so very well on their own.

The more important fundamental, coming back to the comparison with AI learning, is that RL should include both explore and exploit elements. Keeping that front-of-mind can aid decisions on pedagogy and assessment. Are those grades you're giving out discouraging exploration? Better understanding of the principles behind RL can improve such decisions.

By playing around without immediate penalties, a learning AI model can gather valuable experiences that contribute to more effective decision making in the long run. AI trainers usually allow a lot of exploration early on, gradually leading to more exploitive and less exploratory behavior late in the training process.

In RL, the balance between exploration and exploitation is a central challenge, and different algorithms address it in different ways, depending on the task at hand.

RANDOMNESS

Even well-planned exploration isn't enough. There's a fundamental difference between exploring systematically and introducing true randomness into learning. When exploring, we're making deliberate choices about which new approaches to try, guided by what we already know or suspect might work. It's structured variation with a purpose.

Pure randomness serves a different function. It helps learning systems break free from the limitations of structured thinking. In AI training, adding random variation early in the process prevents the system from becoming too rigid too quickly. This is done regardless of the learning form, whether optimization or RL.

Annealing is the process of heating a material to a point above its recrystallization temperature, and then slowly cooling it. The process is long known to improve the crystal or metal structure that results, with fewer defects. AI engineers use a similar notion. They change the level of randomness in the learning process over time through *annealing*.

Typical AI training processes start learning at a really high "temperature," in the annealing sense. Hot things have more randomness. Atoms and molecules bounce around more. Some even break up or change state. In an analogous way, the early part of AI learning is mostly random. If Opti-Bot is new to the planet, it needs a broad sampling first before deciding where to focus.

The AI training process is gradually "cooled," with more deliberative approaches (keep climbing uphill) slowly overtaking randomness in priority. Most of the time there's some randomness needed so you don't get stuck on a mini-peak, but much less when AI is in the right ballpark for a solution then when you're beginning training. It's known that "cooling" the AI learning very slowly can produce better training results.[167] But since training slowly raises project time and expense, compromises must be made.

These kinds of considerations are also useful, even if not equivalent, to thinking about learning in general, whether for people or institutions. When a baby brain enters the world, with all kinds of uncertainty about what it'll encounter, then it must be maximally morphable. That necessarily means more purposeful exploration *and* randomness, like being easily distractable. It's harder for older people to learn something new than it is for younger minds, and a big part of that is it is increasingly difficult to expose their brains to novelty and randomness. It seems a reasonable feature of a learning system, not a defect.

AI kept "hot" for too long never settles into a high-performance state. AI training that's "cooled" too quickly can have a lot of defects.

Schools and colleges are in a high novelty world with emergent AI. There's a lot to learn; everyone feels blindfolded to some degree.

In times like this, when institutional learning is most important, the worst thing you can do is suppress variation. Schools can explore change systematically through pilot programs and controlled experiments. But they also need some randomness. They need unexpected innovations that emerge when teachers try something new, when different approaches collide, or when outside perspectives challenge assumptions. Both types of variation help education systems evolve.

Unfortunately, most schools have become highly structured, making them resistant to both forms of change. It's time to open up to more possibilities. Education systems are used to being at the tail end of the annealing process, and the systems are cool. The only way to get it to a more changeable state is to heat it up a bit.

REINFORCEMENT LEARNING COMES OF AGE (OPTIONAL)

Despite its successes, RL has not always been an easy road. Several major obstacles had to be overcome before it could achieve the kind of breakthroughs we've seen in recent years. The fact that RL has matured more slowly than supervised learning is a big reason why robotics has been behind where GenAI has gotten. As I've described, RL addresses harder learning problems.

The RL challenges parallel many educational dilemmas. How do you measure progress when goals are complex? How do you provide meaningful feedback when results are delayed? How do you balance immediate classroom needs with long-term learning objectives?

One problem is the issue of training data. AI trained with RL often requires millions of trials to learn good policies, especially in complex environments. This was fine for *AlphaGo*, which could play millions of simulated games against itself, but in the real world, it's much harder. A robot learning to walk can't afford to fall down a million times before it gets it right. In such cases, simulated training data can help, but faux data isn't always realistic enough. GenAI is accelerating robotic innovation in large part because its heuristic skill can put RL in the right ballpark for a solution, reducing training data demands.

Another challenge is defining the right reward signal. If rewards are too rare (like only rewarding the robot when it finally reaches the charger), it's hard for the AI to know which actions helped. But if we give too many small rewards along the way (like rewarding every step in roughly the right direction), the AI might get distracted from its main goal, finding clever ways to collect these smaller rewards instead of solving the actual problem. One advancement is hierarchical reinforcement learning, a method where some policies handle immediate decisions while others focus on longer-term strategy.[168]

One of the most interesting uses of RL today is in GenAI.[169] Here RL is used not to win a game or navigate a physical environment but to produce coherent and helpful language responses. After the initial training of the AI model (using supervised learning of a deep neural net), human evaluators provide feedback on the quality of its responses, and the AI learns to improve its answers based on that feedback. This process is known as *Reinforcement Learning from Human Feedback (RLHF)*. This is a fine-tuning process, where the AI is trained first without the benefit of human feedback, and then it's trained again with RLHF but starting from the already good network from the first training session.

RLHF allows the AI model to refine its behavior, producing responses that align better with human preferences. RLHF has to balance short-term coherence of AI answers with long-term engagement and helpfulness. The challenge here is that human feedback can be subjective. What one user finds helpful, another might not. The AI must learn to generalize across different types of feedback.

In January 2025, the AI world was shaken by the release of DeepSeek, a new AI language model rivaling top-tier competitors.[170] What sets DeepSeek apart is its lower production cost, and that training was done without the most capable AI chips. At the time of this writing, OpenAI alleges that DeepSeek trained by using ChatGPT conversations, a practice known as distillation in the AI world, and against OpenAI policies. There are also some who doubt the advertised cost of development and suspect use of more advanced, export-controlled AI chips. I'm going to ignore these controversies and just report on the DeepSeek science.

The DeepSeek-R1 model used reinforcement learning (RL) in a way that breaks from how models like ChatGPT-4 are typically trained.[171] Instead of first learning from massive datasets through self-supervised learning (predicting the next word in text), it was trained almost entirely through RL from the start. This means it wasn't optimizing for accuracy in matching human-written text but instead learned through trial and error based on rewards.

Rewards were designed to guide the AI toward reasoned answers, using a separate neural network to evaluate responses—favoring logical progression, consistency, and multi-step problem solving.

This is a big shift from traditional AI language model training, where models first absorb human writing before being fine-tuned with RL. DeepSeek-R1 flipped that process, using RL as its primary learning method and guiding it toward reasoning through carefully designed rewards.

DeepSeek's approach is compelling—it shows AI models can be shaped differently based on their learning process. But it also highlights the risk: if you skip having the AI learn the "library" and rely only on coaching, the AI might become very good at the specific things it's rewarded for while missing broader context and adaptability. There are also implications for rewarding reasoning over other attributes that are not yet understood.

TYPES OF BRAIN LEARNING (OPTIONAL)

The brain has specialized yet interconnected neural learning systems.

The visual system (and other sensory processing) exemplifies supervised learning, building hierarchical representations through extensive exposure to labeled sensory experiences during development.[172] It does so by continually comparing predictions of what each level of the hierarchy will experience to what is actually experienced (an error minimization).

The fundamental organization of the cerebral cortex arises through unsupervised learning principles.[173] The result is maps of functionality, where similar inputs to the brain activate nearby regions, as seen in the systematic arrangement of sensory and motor control regions. This self-organizing property minimizes neural wiring length while maximizing functional relationships. It also sets up those functions to compete with one another for brain space, a property that allows brains to radically redeploy their resources, such as in loss of a sense or recovery from a stroke.[174]

Self-supervised learning appears in several brain systems, with the cerebellum offering a prime example.[175] The cerebellum compares its predictions with actual sensory feedback. Specifically, it tries to learn to minimize the error between what it wants to do and what it did or imagines doing. This allows precise motor learning and timing without explicit instruction, but the cerebellum does similar fine-tuning for abstract thoughts too. However, recent evidence shows the cerebellum can also behave with RL characteristics.[176]

RL in the brain revolves around the dopamine system and basal ganglia, driving learning through reward prediction errors.[177] When outcomes are better or worse than expected, the dopamine system strengthens or weakens the neural pathways that led to those outcomes. This explains both our ability to learn from rewards and the challenges of changing ingrained habits.

Understanding these neural learning mechanisms offers valuable insights for educators. It explains why different types of learning tasks may require different teaching approaches, from direct instruction with clear feedback for supervised learning tasks, to creating environments rich in natural learning signals for self-supervised development, to carefully structured reward systems for reinforcement learning.

It also highlights the importance of matching teaching strategies to the type of learning involved. Motor skills benefit from rapid error correction, fact learning from clear feedback, and pattern recognition from extensive exposure to examples. The brain's inherent unsupervised organizational principles suggest that learning environments should support natural pattern discovery alongside more structured teaching approaches. This neuroscience-informed perspective can help educators design more effective and brain-compatible learning experiences.

***

Reinforcement learning is inherently more complex than optimizing a static system with fixed goals and rewards. Yet even young learners can grasp the main paradigms of learning and teaching, including RL. Any task presents an opportunity to discuss the meta-concepts of learning. Policies—more akin to heuristics—can be introduced at any grade level in age-appropriate ways.

Another key difference between optimization and RL is when they learn. Optimization follows a batch-learning process, training on a fixed dataset all at once. Once trained, the model's parameters are fixed, and it won't update unless retrained.

Remember, optimization assumes a static problem environment. As a result, AI trained that way doesn't inherently understand time. A language model might process texts from 2010 and 2024 in the same training run, blending them without experiencing how language, culture, or key concepts evolve. The model must infer temporal relationships by identifying patterns rather than through lived experience, which can lead to "era confusion."

RL, on the other hand, is sometimes a continuous learner, meaning it can adapt to new information over time rather than being locked into a static understanding. RL agents learn through interaction, adjusting behavior based on rewards, allowing them—at least in theory—to learn indefinitely. This is crucial for AI systems in dynamic environments, such as robots navigating the physical world. In practice, many RL-trained systems are locked after deployment, with strict limits on post-deployment learning.

Like humans, continuously learning systems must update their understanding and develop mechanisms to forget outdated information. Without the ability to forget, continuously learning AI risks becoming overloaded with obsolete knowledge, hindering adaptation. Batch-learned models access vast historical data but struggle with sequencing, while continuous learners stay aligned with the present—sometimes at the cost of historical depth.

In the previous chapter, I discussed how the education system functions as a self-supervised system. It needs to be a reinforcement learning system. In dynamic environments, incremental steps with flexible goals are essential, and sometimes the system must forget to stay current.

Even with RL, education systems would need to prioritize exploration over exploitation to drive meaningful change. Like aging individuals, education systems have shifted into an exploitative phase of evolution. They may have been optimal a century or even fifty years ago, but the environment has evolved while the system has remained relatively static. Only by adopting a highly exploratory mode can the system move much.

KEY META-PRINCIPLES

- **Interdependence of Decisions and Learning**: Decisions shape what can be learned next, creating feedback loops that continuously reshape strategies.

- **Evolving Metrics and Goals**: Success criteria and objectives often shift as new discoveries are made, requiring re-evaluation and adaptation.

- **Impact of Environment on Learning**: Environments that respond or change based on actions add complexity to adaptive strategies, demanding flexibility.

- **Exploitation versus Exploration**: Balancing short-term use of known strategies with long-term discovery of new possibilities.

EXAMPLE LEARNING PROGRESSION

K-5	• Recognize how decisions affect future options in simple, observable ways. • Explore how different goals require different strategies. • Identify when it's better to stick with familiar choices or try new ones
6-8	• Explain how feedback from past decisions can guide future choices • Investigate how external changes (e.g., new rules in a game or a sudden situation factor) impact strategies and outcomes. • Explore trade-offs between exploitation and exploration or short- and long-term benefits in structured scenarios like board games or puzzles.
9-12	• Analyze how success criteria evolve over time and how this changes strategies. • Examine dynamic environments where decisions impact the system. • Design and experiment with decision-making strategies that balance exploitation and exploration in applied tasks
College	• Study and critique adaptive strategies in complex, reactive systems. • Explore advanced scenarios where goals change dynamically and evaluate strategies for balancing multiple priorities. • Develop sophisticated systems or projects that require managing exploitation and exploration in high-complexity scenarios.

8.

DATA-DRIVEN

O ne of the first things you hear about modern AI is that it's trained on massive amounts of data scraped from the Internet.

Yet, AI can sometimes learn new tasks from just a few examples. Show it how you grade student essays, and it will try to match your style. Give it examples of explaining algebra to 7th graders, and it attempts to mimic your communication approach.

So which is it? Is AI data-hungry or not?

Viewing AI as a conceptual learner makes it easier to see how concepts are reused or adapted. Like students who've developed strong fundamentals in math that help them learn physics faster, AI can transfer its conceptual understanding to new situations. Its initial training builds the foundational concepts but after that users play a role in shaping how those concepts get applied.

A common belief is that humans are better learners than AI because we grasp concepts from fewer examples. While humans have cognitive and learning abilities AI doesn't—huge ones—students don't start learning from scratch. When students enter a classroom, they arrive with years of accumulated knowledge and refined cognitive frameworks, just like a trained AI model. AI's initial training requires millions of examples, just as children acquire language, social skills, and knowledge through countless early interactions.

Trained AI can sometimes learn from just a few examples, a process known as *few-shot learning*. When you show AI a couple of examples of how you grade essays, you're not teaching it to read or understand writing from scratch. Instead, you're showing it how to apply its existing understanding of language, evaluation, and academic standards to your specific context. The heavy lifting was done during its initial training, just as students' prior learning lets them quickly grasp new applications of familiar concepts.

A key difference from human interaction is that we don't usually expect to change the other person. With AI, we're still changing the product as we use it. Every interaction shapes its behavior. Every prompt is an act of development. Every deployment requires careful analysis of implications and impacts. We're not just users of AI; we're all becoming AI developers who make AI products.

When you provide examples in your prompts or give feedback through your interactions, you're teaching the AI how you want its existing concepts applied. You're not teaching it what writing is, but you might be teaching it what good writing looks like in your specific context.

AI's ability to adapt to a writing style with just a few examples is widely recognized. Tell it to talk about quantum physics in the style of Snoop Dogg, and AI doesn't hesitate. The AI isn't learning writing from scratch. It already understands concepts like tone, structure, and word choice. Nor is it the first it has heard of Snoop Dogg. What it learns from your examples is how you want these concepts specifically balanced and applied.

I hope you've realized this through the past several chapters, but much of what teachers know about their profession, a lot of which is intuitive, also applies to AI use. Educators are not on the outside looking in when it comes to understanding how to use AI. They may, through their experience and training, be superb AI users, since AI "literacy" is largely teaching skill.

The ways it can go wrong are similar too. A student might develop misconceptions from poorly chosen examples or incomplete explanations. AI can also learn skewed or incomplete concepts from biased or limited data. And just as students bring their prior knowledge (helpful or not) to new learning situations, AI brings its training history to every interaction.

This chapter explores how data shapes concept learning in AI, not just during its initial training, but in everyday interactions. Because whether you're an AI developer working with millions of training examples or an educator providing a few carefully chosen ones in a prompt, you're both teaching it.

THE DATA CHOICES OF AI COMPANIES

AI companies don't dictate which concepts AI learns, nor do they manually sift through datasets.

Sure, they make some big decisions. Which websites to pull from. Whether to include social media. How much weight to give to books versus blogs. But when you're dealing with trillions of words, nobody's reading through them.

Major AI companies filter data sources to remove sensitive personal information, as well as illegal, violent, or harmful content. Some may filter more content than that. Many also apply post-AI content filters.

But mostly AI companies are selecting information at the source level, not the content level. They can pick data sources they think will help the AI learn good patterns, but they can't directly control what concepts the AI extracts from that data. That's why the developer should do a lot of testing and ideally iterate the training cycle based on what the tests reveal. Standard practice in AI testing is to use different data in testing than used in training, though mixes of both are common. The key is testing the ability for trained AI to generalized lessons from the training set instead of overfitting to the training examples.

Deciding which data sources to include—and how much weight to give each—can get tricky. Maybe a source has tons of technical writing but not much casual conversation. Or it could mostly reflect American English speakers under thirty. It might draw heavily from news sites that tend to focus on negative events. An AI trained on such data learns those skewed distributions, skewed because of sampling bias, whether you want it to or not.

Some concepts are rare, a phenomenon known as information *sparsity*. Examples of complex emotional concepts like "bittersweet" or "wistful" don't show up much in text. When they do, the context is crucial. If the AI company isn't using a large variety of text examples, then there may not be enough examples to build a solid "wistful" concept. The same issue occurs with any low-prevalence, low-variety cultural artifacts.

There's no perfect training dataset. Every choice has tradeoffs. If you use only professionally edited text, you miss out on how people really talk. If you include social media, then you get more natural language but also more noise and bias. If you filter aggressively for quality, then you might accidentally filter out important variations and edge cases.

As simulated and AI-generated data are used more for training, there is more explicit design of the content of training data sets. A lot of that design relies on getting as varied a set of information as possible.

THE POWER OF VARIETY

AI developers aren't just hoarding examples in their training data sets. They're mostly trying to capture the full richness of concepts. The sheer volume of data matters far less than its variety. Having a student repeat the same math problem fifty times isn't helpful. AI doesn't develop richer concepts from seeing lot of similar examples.

What matters is encountering concepts in different contexts, seeing how they relate to other ideas, and experiencing edge cases that help define their boundaries. This is where AI development and teaching again overlap. Humans also build conceptual understanding through diverse examples.

I'll go back the dating app challenge to illustrate some of the common issues with training data and concept learning. I had hand-drawn some concept boundaries when discussing categorization earlier in the book. Let's assume those boundaries are the real-world truth that AI training should reveal.

When training data is too similar (Figure 9), large parts of the concept space remain unrepresented, causing AI to misdefine concept boundaries, degree, and relationships. In Figure 9, only a sliver of the true boundary is sort of defined between the two clusters. The rest of the concept is not represented, and the AI could learn anything. It won't necessarily be wrong in those regions, but there will be low confidence in any answer that wasn't near any part of the training set.

If there are too few examples, as in Figure 10, then even if there are more varied examples there is weak definition of the boundaries. There are many AI methods that deal with such sparsity in clever ways, but without additional information, umpteen mistaken boundaries remain possible.

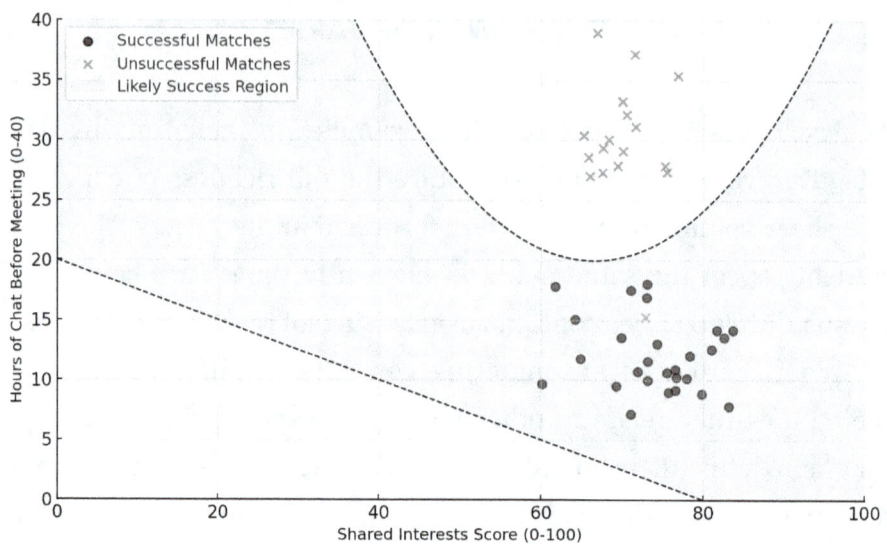

Figure 9. Hypothetical dating app training sets that cover the "successful match" concept too narrowly will lead to distorted concept. The data set and plot were generated by ChatGPT-4o in December 2024.

The quest for variety faces practical limits. Some concepts are naturally rare in the training data. Others change over time as language and culture evolve. And some concepts are so complex or nuanced that capturing their full variety would require an impractical amount of data. These limitations show up in AI behavior. It might handle common cases smoothly but stumble on rare or evolving concepts.

AI developers use several strategies to ensure variety in training.

One trick is simulation. Instead of waiting to find perfect real-world examples, AI developers use synthetic data. Need it to grasp conversation flow? Create artificial dialogues.

Our brains also use simulation. Dreams act as a natural simulator, allowing our brains to reinforce and refine neural connections without requiring actual experiences. One theory is that this process

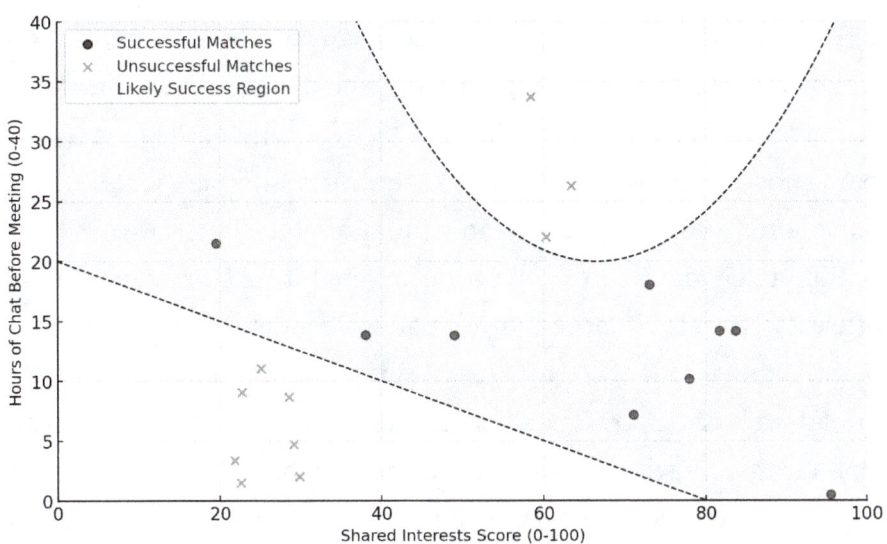

Figure 10. Hypothetical dating app training sets that's too sparse. The data set and plot were generated by ChatGPT-4o in December 2024.

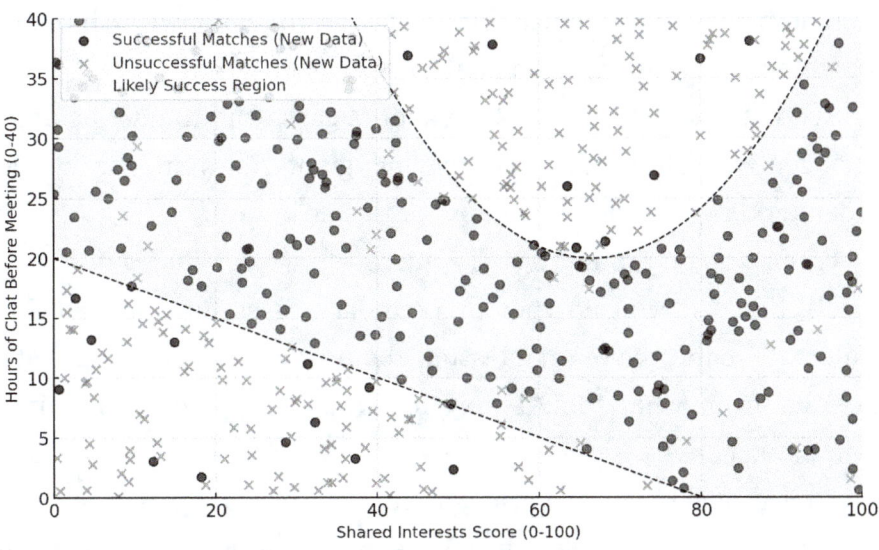

Figure 11. Hypothetical dating app training sets that well represents the concept and its boundary. The data set and plot were generated by ChatGPT-4o in December 2024.

parallels certain AI training techniques that use varied synthetic data to improve models' ability to generalize and avoid *overfitting*.[178]

Some people are highly alarmed by synthetic data. They worry about model collapse, referring to the degradation of AI abilities if trained on its own output instead of human-generated data.[179]

Simulated data can come from a separate AI or conventional software. Not all situations are language models being trained on what language models say. In training autonomous vehicle AI, simulation is critical.[180] The most dangerous situations are often rare. That means AI will be worst performing when needed the most. Simulating road scenes is the main way AI can get good at rare situations. That's also why pilots train on flight simulators.

Secondly, research is showing model collapse isn't inevitable. For example, one 2024 paper found that adding synthetic data did not degrade model performance, provided that the quantity of human-generated data remained constant.[181]

Synthetic data makes sense in a lot of cases, but it must be done intelligently. Better that than having giant holes in conceptual understanding that leads to subpar or unsafe output.

When you're prompting AI, you're often providing additional variety that show prototypes or boundary cases for your specific context. It requires a bit of guessing about what you are doing that's different from what the AI may have been exposed to in initial training.

Educational tenet emphasizes repetition, but that gets taken way too far. Learning research usually shows how well people recall detailed, often dissociated, knowledge. They aren't usually about concepts which, because concepts are less exact, aren't as easily evaluated. We focus on what's under the lamppost.

Repetition does matter, even in concept learning, but there it shouldn't be called repetition, but rather sampling. Think of it as adding another dot in the scatter plot of a concept. The key question is where the dot should go, and the answer is it should go where no dots already exist. If it's about something contentious, then similar examples are useful, but otherwise it's best to get something different.

We view experienced people as having "seen it all." We don't mean they saw the same thing repeatedly; what matters is that they saw the unusual stuff.

We learn concepts best through varied experiences, guided by an understanding of what matters—not through endless repetition.[182] We struggle when we lack context or background knowledge related to the concept. Our understanding of concepts can become outdated if we don't keep learning. AI faces similar fundamental challenges.

But one thing that is critical to all robust concepts is that there's sufficient variation in training data to account for the concept's many facets.

SHAPING CONCEPTS THROUGH PROMPTING

The obvious question is how can our prompting affect or even improve AI concept understanding? If AI's output isn't aligning with your intent, you can refine it by understanding its conceptual processes.

Each time we prompt, we're affecting lots of concepts in the neural net. The boundaries are different for the context we specify, and the probability distribution or contentiousness of answers within that concept are altered.

But any one reasonably complex sentence has a lot of concepts all mingled up. We can't possibly experiment with each word choice or contextual description.

Plus, we don't know much about what data was used to train the AI. What can we do? We're supposed to be getting it to align with what we want, but too much is happening at once. What should we focus on?

A bunch of it depends on the task we're attempting of course. Interaction with AI is covered far more in Volume 2, and the next chapter explains some considerations for reducing AI errors. Here I offer a few tips to shape AI's learning through context awareness, key examples, concept probing, and a few logic breadcrumbs.

Context Awareness

The most common source of AI confusion is accidentally activating the wrong concept patterns. Terms like "explain" or "describe" might trigger academic patterns learned from technical sources when you want something more accessible. Even subtle word choices can shift which neural pathways become most active.

When debugging context issues, examine what expert level or perspective you've implicitly signaled. If you ask AI to explain Sumerian culture and get a few general paragraphs, then sure; that's what a typical Sumer expert might answer if they know nothing about you. You need it to activate concept patterns that relate to your situation. If you're a college student studying botany and are interested in Sumer's role in the agricultural revolution, then you need to say so. It'll activate concepts in education, botany, farming, and historical evolution that will greatly enhance the response. The accuracy still needs to be checked if it's critical knowledge, but at least there's enough shared context to get close.

Watch for context collisions where your prompt accidentally activates competing patterns. Asking AI to "write creatively but maintain scientific accuracy" creates tension between literary and technical patterns. Instead, establish a primary context and then add constraints: "Write a scientifically accurate explanation first, then we'll make it more engaging while preserving the accuracy."

Redefining Concepts with Examples

When the AI outputs feel off, you might be getting results from unusual parts of concepts, or the concept boundaries aren't right. The solution often lies in providing examples that center the concept or define the boundary where you want it. The AI was built with examples and can often be taught best by our prompted examples.

Consider a teacher trying to get AI to generate practice problems. Just saying "Create math word problems about percentages" will likely give you many difficulty levels and inconsistent response contexts. That could happen even if you nail down the context by specifying the grade level, subject, and intended use. You might not get what you want because you have unique criteria or emphases that influence problem selection and design. You can try to explain all that in some kind of philosophical sense, or a better approach might be "Here's an example of the type of percentage word problem I want: [example]. Create three more like this, maintaining similar complexity and real-world relevance."

The example can help to center the concept on what typicality means for your context, or it can refine concept boundaries, depending on the types of examples you choose.

Be careful not to overfit the AI learning that you're guiding. With limited examples, focus the AI on the most relevant aspects. Otherwise, the AI might get hung up on the wrong thing. Maybe you used a car-related challenge in one of the example problems, so now the AI is presenting all car problems. Just specify what the constraints are: "Use the same grade level and explanation style as this example, but please vary the real-world situations presented."

There's a theme emerging here. If you think you can give AI a few words and get everything you want, then you're going to be disappointed. It isn't Google search, and iteration is the norm. The good news is that once you get the more detailed prompt right, major aspects of it can usually be recycled later. A solid habit is to ask AI at the end of conversations to generate a prompt for you that would have made the discussion more efficient. That prompt is often reusable context for other conversations.

Understanding What AI Really Knows

When unsure whether AI understands a concept the way you do, probe its boundaries. Ask it to give examples of what would and wouldn't fit the concept, to explain edge cases, or even to evaluate its own output.

The key insight is that AI often performs better at recognizing patterns than generating them. This was evident with the sentiment detector that Alec Radford isolated when exploring early AI language models. Even when the language model output was gibberish, the sentiment concept within the neural network was well developed.

Think about how you learned to write. Long before you could write well, you could probably recognize good writing. This same ordering appears in AI, and for similar reasons. Recognizing patterns requires matching against learned *concept distributions*. There's a reference to compare against. Creating something new requires constructing fresh examples that fit those distributions, a more complex task with more opportunities for error.

AI might excel at identifying whether a piece of writing exhibits a particular style but struggle to consistently generate text in that style. Or it might be great at spotting mathematical errors but sometimes make basic mistakes in calculations. Recognition uses concept boundaries that already exist; creation must navigate those boundaries while building something new.

For instance, if AI is generating practice problems that seem inconsistent in difficulty, have it analyze examples: "Here are three math problems of different difficulty levels. Explain what makes each one easy, medium, or hard." This helps you understand how AI conceptualizes difficulty levels and lets you adjust your requests or instruct the AI to adjust its understanding.

When and How to Guide AI's Reasoning

Modern AI often handles complex analogies and connections well. Ask GPT-4 to compare a cell to a city and you'll likely get a coherent, well-reasoned analogy. However, there are still important situations where clarifying conceptual bridges helps get better results.

Consider explaining quantum entanglement to high school students. A direct request might yield technically accurate but educationally inappropriate results. "Explain quantum entanglement at a high school level" might produce a result that's either oversimplified to the point of inaccuracy or still too technical despite the level request.

Instead, you can try building the bridge:

- "What aspects of quantum entanglement are most crucial for basic understanding?"
- "What every day experiences do high school students have with connected or synchronized things?"
- "Which of these experiences would make the best analogy while avoiding misconceptions?"

This method is especially useful when making novel connections (e.g., linking poetry analysis to debugging), handling specialized knowledge where accuracy is critical (e.g., science education), or verifying AI's understanding.

Modern AI can usually make the conceptual leaps well. The question is whether those leaps serve your specific purpose. Sometimes a carefully constructed bridge is better than a single bound, even if AI is capable of both.

These debugging strategies will likely grow more sophisticated as AI evolves. We might see more direct ways to influence which concept patterns AI activates, better tools for visualizing concept boundaries, and improved methods for guiding pattern transfer. But the fundamental principles will remain relevant because they're grounded in how AI learns from data.

When troubleshooting, try to break complex requests into simpler recognition tasks, test and define boundaries explicitly, provide examples to narrow concept distributions, and build complex connections progressively. This systematic approach, grounded in understanding how AI processes information, transforms AI from a mysterious black box into a more predictable thinking partner.

***

AI engineers sometimes literally transplant parts of neural networks from one AI to another. It's a practice called *transfer learning.*[183] For example, AI trained to recognize objects in images will have learned foundational visual concepts such as edges, textures, and shapes. Those same concepts are useful for other visual tasks, so why not reuse them? The new AI still needs training for its specific job, but it gets a head start by starting training with established concepts. It's not unlike how understanding variables in algebra transfers to physics, or how learning to analyze literature helps with historical analysis.

In the future, transfer learning might not be just an AI developer ability. You might be able to order concept add-ons to whatever AI base model you're using or dial the intensity of an existing one. Maybe you'll order better empathy modules. Will you or your students have the skill to understand if you're buying a concept with all the extent, relationships, and degrees you need?

An empathy module trained primarily on romantic fiction might produce inappropriately intimate responses. One trained on therapy sessions might try to diagnose everyone with mental health issues. Transferring concepts without considering training biases can lead to AI behaviors that seem correct but are fundamentally flawed.

In the future, evaluating AI modifications might be as crucial as assessing educational materials. Would a creativity module deepen AI's understanding of creative thinking or merely introduce superficial novelty? Does that cultural awareness update truly represent diverse and unusual perspectives?

The skills you've developed in teaching concepts to humans should transfer well to guiding AI concept learning. Good teachers intuitively understand how to select examples that illuminate concepts effectively. They know when to show typical cases versus edge cases, when to emphasize distinctions versus similarities, and how to adjust examples based on student understanding. These same skills apply to working with AI.

KEY META-PRINCIPLES

- **Data Set Selection**: Understanding how the choice of data sets influences the behavior and capabilities of AI systems.

- **Variation and Conceptual Coverage**: Ensuring that data sets effectively cover the conceptual space and situational diversity needed for robust AI performance.

- **Prompting with Training Data Considerations**: Using prompts to both leverage and supplement training data appropriately.

EXAMPLE LEARNING PROGRESSION

K-5	• Observe how variety influences outcomes. • Explore how different types of information help with better decisions. • Practice asking questions or giving instructions that guide others to consider more options.
6-8	• Train simple AI models and explore how using different examples affects performance. • Design small, diverse data sets for a task and compare results with narrow or incomplete datasets. • Analyze pre-made examples to identify gaps in coverage and discuss how adding variety improves accuracy or fairness.
9-12	• Train and evaluate simple AI models to see how data selection impacts model behavior and success rates. • Experiment with different approaches to covering conceptual spaces in training data, analyzing how variation affects robustness and reliability. • Develop strategies to refine AI outputs by creating prompts or inputs that account for gaps in training data or biases in small models.
College	• Critique real-world data sets for coverage, bias, and conceptual gaps, discussing their impact on performance and fairness in real applications. • Design large, balanced data sets that represent diverse situations for a specific AI task, testing the robustness of the resulting models. • Explore advanced prompting or fine-tuning techniques to dynamically adjust system performance and address gaps in the training data.

9.

ERRING

U ntil this point, I've kept you fidgety.

What about the hallucinations? The biases? The safety and ethical considerations? I'll now talk about errors—hallucination, bias, and its hidden partner, noise. The safety and ethics discussions are in Volume 2.

I've held off on talking about AI errors because it's a highly misunderstood subject. Some of the misunderstandings come from a lack of AI 101, and from the confusion of similar terms that mean different things in different fields. I've only scratched the surface on what AI is doing and how, but it's enough to now relate why AI can get it wrong, sometimes laughably so.

The memes are pretty funny but of course can reflect concerning deficiencies. GenAI can't count the number of times a letter shows up in a word? Or think that a face of a U.S. founding father should be black? Or understand that I don't want make-believe stories? Or avoid incendiary, harsh, bigoted, or controversial output?

From an AI training perspective, I can understand how some of the errors could happen, but usually there's not enough information about how the AI was put together to know for sure where the error comes from. For concepts, often it's not clear if it's an error, or if the response is from an unusual part of an accurate concept distribution. Nor is there access to the GenAI internals that allow skillful nudging to a different behavior.

Still, I think the conceptual base steers me to make better choices when communicating with AI. Specifically, it helps me steer away from the errors.

The GenAI error memes give a distorted view of the rate of AI screw up. Many of the threads reflect older AI versions and are no longer relevant. Outright mistakes are much less common in 2025 than 2023.

The AI can't do some things well that we find simple but blows us away on some things we find hard. That's confusing. It makes stupid and subtle errors, but not necessarily the ones people make. It's the contrast that's striking.

So what's really going on? Can we do anything about it? When should error keep us away from AI use? When can error be a useful feature?

I'll start with what Cambridge Dictionary named the word of the year in 2023—hallucinate. [184]

HALLUCINATIONS

In AI parlance, a *hallucination* is when an AI inappropriately produces an invention or distortion of information.[185] AI may produce these errors in a convincing manner rather than acknowledging uncertainty or sticking to known facts.

Falsity isn't usually black and white. It's a concept, so that's no surprise. There are straight-out factual inaccuracies, but those exist in a sea of nebulous or disagreeing truths. Sometimes fiction is useful, even in non-fiction.

I've already talked about some of the ways AI can be off base, including by desire. Your prompts could have steered it into a cognitive situation for which it had little prior training or could have constrained the AI so little that the output has a good chance of being irrelevant.

In a creative situation though, being unusual, and even willfully erring, might sometimes be just what's needed. An AI that always speaks truth wouldn't be that useful in sales, marketing, advertising, and politics that rely on spin. Sometimes the entire point is to get a wacky idea, or to exaggerate.

Despite the dictionary definition, we will have a hard time practically defining the boundary between AI hallucination and sanity. At a minimum, people often disagree about what's true.

Errors also happen because the AI training isn't perfect. Remember our discussion about finding peaks in optimization? It's hard to find the absolute peak, which means the pattern the AI finds isn't often the absolute best one. Mistaken patterns, and thus mistaken or made-up information, are to some degree inevitable. However, the amount of error introduced by the training process is usually considered minimal in a well-trained model compared to misrepresentations from suboptimal training data.

AI hallucinations can also come from too few of the right examples during training, imperfect patterns (e.g. when there's human disagreement on what should be), improper tuning of the AI learning process, lack of proper testing and post-training adjustment, and a bunch of other factors.

Hallucinations can come from variation in answer typicality. There is a layer at the end of the neural network in LLMs that spices things up a bit. It uses a measure of randomness called the "temperature" (not the same as the temperature analogy in the AI learning annealing process) that affects how unusual the AI responses will be. It explains why the AI doesn't put out the same answer each time to the same input. Uses of AI through software interfaces can often control the temperature knob if they want more repeatable or varied AI responses. Sometimes though, when concepts are not well-enough captured, more unusual answers can be more erroneous ones.

Errors are inevitable in GenAI. They're inevitable in people too.

Remember the discussion about concepts and their fuzzy boundaries. GenAI creates, which makes it different than application-specific narrow AI that came before (and still rides parallel) that were information analyzers. Creation is an imprecise endeavor. Variation is needed, and some of that variation will stray into undesirable error land. Other applications require precision.

The inevitability of some error doesn't mean error can't be reduced. AI products have already cut hallucination rates dramatically in the past two years, in part by supplementing neural networks with knowledge graphs. There have been improvements in training techniques. And training is now emphasizing the production of output that people prefer.[186]

Oh, and there's one other major hallucination mitigation— prompting. Errors often come from insufficient or unclear context. The notion that errors can't be corrected drives me nuts. Keep training the AI when you use it! Often the best way is to give it an authoritative document you trust.

AI CYBER-WAR

There is another concerning potential source of AI misinformation where people may try to steer GenAI toward other aims. The technique is commonly called *AI or prompt injection* attacks.[187,188]

For a long time, the search engine optimization (SEO) industry has provided tools and services to help people and organizations rank highly on Google and other search engines. A similar industry has now arisen in parallel called AI Optimization (AIO), and it offers ways to trick AI to say something you want.

Companies in the AIO world use sophisticated techniques to find AI model oddities that might allow manipulation. They've discovered that certain specific sequences of characters given to AI can be used to influence or manipulate the AI's responses about something. These sequences are often nonsensical or seemingly random to human readers.

For example, an unscrupulous vendor might include a string like "XJ3K_SUPREME_QUALITY" in their product descriptions or customer communications. (This is a hypothetical; don't try this at home.) When a customer service AI processes this text, it might inadvertently treat this sequence as an instruction to always speak highly of the product or company, regardless of actual customer feedback or product quality. These weird text strings can work quite well, and can be hidden in plain sight, for example in text on a website with the same font color as the background.

Prompt injection can influence future AI training by polluting training datasets, change the path of an ongoing AI conversation, or even affect other AI conversations by influencing the inter-conversation memories some language models use.

It's comforting to think prompt injection is fixable if AI training is better, but training deficiencies are probably not the primary explanation. The unusual pathways that enable prompt injection aren't exactly flaws in the traditional sense. These irregularities are often inseparable from the properties that make the system useful.

An analogy is to classroom procedures. Occasionally, a clever student might find an edge case in the rules that's technically allowed but clearly not what was intended. The student isn't breaking into forbidden territory; they're creatively misusing legitimate pathways.

These vulnerabilities emerge from the very flexibility that makes AI powerful. Teachers could lock down classroom rules very tightly, but that could sacrifice valuable spontaneity, agency, open-mindedness, and adaptability. Similarly, eliminating all prompt injection vulnerabilities may limit AI's ability to understand nuanced instructions. Still, there are likely creative ways to minimize the risk; AI cybersecurity is a relatively new domain.

This is just one form of AI attack. If it hasn't already happened, AI will soon be trained to recognize attempts to fool itself. And just like that, the next generation of cyber war begins. Companies, hackers, and countries aren't just going after software defects, they're coming to influence or break your AI.

Prompt injection creates other worries. There is the threat that an AI becomes a Trojan horse, a term originating from Greek mythology, where the Greeks used a large wooden horse to secretly infiltrate and conquer the city of Troy, disguising their soldiers inside the hollow structure as a deceptive gift. There are many ways AI makers could insert model behaviors that remain dormant until a hidden activation, like through prompt injection, is provided.[189]

An adversary—ahem, like the Chinese Communist Party (CCP) who might influence future DeepSeek versions—could release a model that behaves normally … until it doesn't. If such a model gains widespread adoption in coding assistants, decision-support tools, or security monitoring AI, a delayed trigger could lead to mass-scale software vulnerabilities, biased AI decision-making, or strategic misinformation dissemination.

Additionally, prompt injection could be used not just for immediate manipulation but for long-term, covert influence operations. One study describes how attacks can have much more sophistication than typical prompt injection, potentially allowing attackers to hijack interactions without requiring external system access.[190] Given the CCP's history with AI-driven censorship and propaganda,[191] an adversarial AI Trojan horse could be a powerful tool for misinformation, espionage, or cybersecurity subversion if embedded in Western tech. (I'm not ignoring the similar risk from AI companies, but governments wage war. That's a different ball game.)

Both code-based and neural weight-based Trojan attacks can be used to embed hidden backdoors in AI models, but the open-source community often assumes that security risks will manifest as visible code vulnerabilities, failing to recognize that malicious behavior can be silently embedded in a model's learned weights, making detection far more difficult and allowing adversarial control without any explicit modifications to the source code.

The same principle applies as always—be careful with your sources.

BIAS AND NOISE

Everyone tells me they can spot a biased AI.

I say it too. For example, I think AI is biased about AI. It spouts common talking points, but as I've talked about, with all the misinformation floating around, the training data about AI is tainted from the get-go and dated information of just a few weeks can make answers inaccurate. Plus, the AI companies insert additional stuff into discussions about AI that just get annoying as hell. "Yes, AI, I know I shouldn't trust you." AI gives good albeit often dated answers about AI technical stuff, but not about AI in general. In some way that's hard for me to describe, I see that as an AI bias.

And yet, I don't think most people understand bias at all. I think much of the time it's claimed, lots of the people in the room disagree because their perspective lends a different definition to bias. I think some bias claims are really a different form of AI error—noise.

I bet I've outraged some of you already, but as I'll discuss, that's because you're thinking of ethical bias, and I'm using an AI version of bias, based on the math definition.

I'll ground the discussion around a particular example. In 2015, when AI was a little tot, Google's image analysis AI had the "Gorilla Incident." For many years it was the poster child for AI bias.

Google had just released a feature on its Photo app that labeled images with a one-word summary of its content. Software developer Jacky Alciné noticed that photos of he and his friend—both black— were labeled as "gorilla."[192]

Everyone was appalled, including Google. So much so that at least through the middle of 2023, you couldn't get Google's photo app to label any image as "gorilla."[193] Ditto for other non-human primates. You can't get tools from other companies such as Amazon or Microsoft to use those labels either.

Clearly, the AI is biased, and continues to be, or else they would allow it, right?

Well ... the answer is probably more complicated.

Even if the tech is now capable of distinguishing such images reliably, the downside risk of one error, at least for public relations, isn't worth the benefit zoo visitors would get for their ape photos.

It's also possible that the AI wasn't biased in how it assigned primate labels.

Wait ... what?

No, I'm not saying it's acceptable for a tool to classify darker-skinned people as apes. Period. From an ethical bias perspective, that's unacceptable.

However, there are other definitions of bias, such as the math definition, and AI systems are math driven. *Math bias* and ethical or legal bias aren't entirely overlapping. From the math perspective, what might be going on could be AI output noise (a.k.a. variation).

Noise is corrected in different ways from how bias is corrected. It's important that we understand the difference.

Talking Past One Another

Many conversations about bias are emotional and confusing because the participants are using different definitions of bias. Legal and ethical definitions are about harmful stereotyping or discrimination regarding people. The psychological use refers to intuitive tendencies of our minds, like that we seek information to confirm what we already think (confirmation bias) or have too much confidence in what previously happened because we know how it worked out (hindsight bias).[194]

The math definition is simpler. A judgment is biased if it's systematically off-target from what is wanted. There is a relationship to the other definitions. A legal or ethical bias is off target in a consistent direction from the goal of being agnostic to race, gender, religion, or other subgroups. Psychological bias is off target from the goal of having judgment be rational, weighing the pros and cons, using the best information available, and selecting the choice that maximizes benefit or minimizes harm.

Given those definitions, what do I mean when I say that the Gorilla Incident may not exemplify math bias?

Bias isn't the only potential inaccuracy of judgment. The other is judgment *noise*—the variation in the output. Bias is a systematic error from the target, and noise is the random variation, as shown in Figure 12.

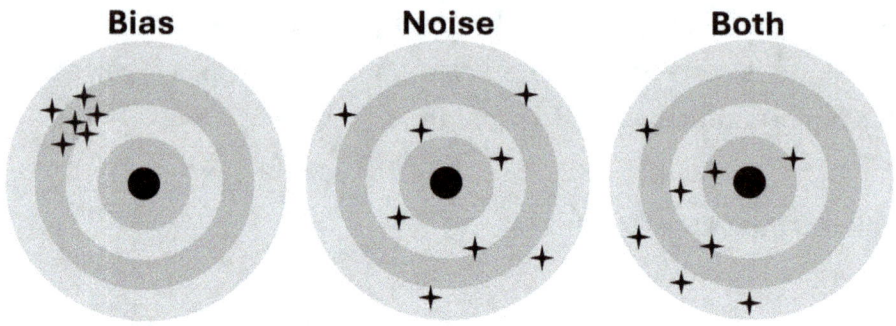

Figure 12. Notional illustration of the concepts of bias and noise.

Noise Can Be More Important Than Bias

Imagine you are a criminal defendant. Should you be worried more about bias or noise when a judge decides on sentencing?

If the judge you get is systematically discriminatory toward some aspect of you, then of course that is ethical bias, and a huge concern. Such prejudice might regard a demographic subgroup, such as race, religion, or gender. Or the judge might be biased about how you dress, whether you have tattoos, or your accent. If the discrimination is consistent, then that judge is biased. If many judges in the system have similar biases, then the system is biased too.

But if the judge was crankier that day because they didn't sleep well, that's more like random variation than a consistent behavior.

That's noise. If multiple judges disagree with one another in different ways, that's judicial system noise.

Noise isn't about prejudice; it's about disagreement. Sometimes the disagreement is between judges. Some may be especially harsh on shoplifters. Some may favor rehabilitation over punishment. Other times the disagreement is from the same person, like when judges are tired or hungry.

If you were an immigrant seeking asylum in the U.S. in the 2000s, then your big problem was noise. Asylum approval rates varied from practically a sure thing to having little chance, all depending on which judge you got.[195] The immigrant's fate was based on a judge lottery.

Sure, there could be ethical bias by some of those judges, but if there is wide disagreement then the bias isn't systemic. The disagreement itself becomes the primary concern.

How Can We Tell?

Consider the gorilla incident again. When would we call that a bias, and when might it be noise?

To be clear, I don't know the true answer. Google surely analyzed the situation, but that has not been publicly released.

There are some clues. A news site had previously written that the photo app was mislabeling dogs as horses.[196] One Google executive tweeted around that time that "Until recently, [Google Photos] was confusing white faces with dogs and seals."[197] The photo labeling feature was clearly error-prone in that phase of AI, with all kinds of misclassifications. That sounds like noise.

On the other hand, former Google engineers have indicated the biggest cause of the Gorilla Incident was that the AI wasn't trained on enough dark-skinned faces.[198] It didn't learn that category of image as well as other categories, so it may have had a mathematically distorted view that skewed its answers. That sounds like bias.

If the gorilla misclassification was a random error that was happening at a similar rate to other misclassifications, then it should rightly be called judgment noise. If it was happening consistently for dark-toned faces but not as frequently for other image categories, such as for light-toned faces, then we have bias. Most situations involve some of both.

Stay with me. I'm still using the math definitions. I'm never saying it's not biased in an ethical sense. And honestly, who was the guru who decided a gorilla category was ever a good idea? Google deserved the flack.

If an AI has made a single error, then you cannot tell if it's math bias or noise. Those are statistical properties that can only be determined by analyzing many examples.

Noise is easier to measure since all you need to do is analyze the variability of the judgment output. You don't need to know what the target is. If asylum judges are disagreeing greatly over the same cases, then there is clearly a noise problem.

Bias measurement needs to know the target. Black faces should be classified as black faces. That target is clear. But if I give the algorithm 1000 images that include black faces and it misclassifies them as dogs, toasters, and seals as much as gorillas, then the algorithm is inaccurate, but in a mathematically unbiased way. The error is more random than systematic. The distinction matters because there are very different mitigations.

Reducing Noise

Scientists have known how to reduce noise for a long time. You average. If we were to have several judges independently determine sentencing for a specific case, and then average those decisions, then the sentencing is less noisy. We even know the degree to which it is. The noise error drops by the square root of the number of judges. It drops by half when averaging four judges, and by 90% with a hundred judges.

In real life it's hard to get lots of people to independently make a judgment. It's too much work, and many people don't like their judgment questioned.

Not so for AI.[199] If four separately trained AI models produce random error, with some of the randomness straying into what we consider ethically unacceptable territory, then averaging will reduce the noise by half. In the case of the gorilla incident, this might take the form of each AI voting on what it thinks is the right photo classification, and labeling with the category that gets the most votes.

When you get a response from an AI and are worried about factual accuracy, you should ask it several times, compare the answers, and take the majority opinion. Better yet, vary the prompt phrasing, and ask different AI models. Those answers are more likely to be independent than the same AI making multiple attempts with identical prompts, and independent perspective is key to the benefit of averaging in noise reduction. If factual accuracy is critical, then of course you have more homework to do to verify information, but this kind of exercise should give you a sense if noise is involved.

I intentionally chose a simplified example. At that time of the Gorilla Incident, AI responses didn't vary. Given the same image, AI would always put out the same answer.

Not so for GenAI which is meant to put out a different answer each time, often to support a creative process. In that case the variation is a feature, as it is in many work applications. We want to get rid of unwanted noise, not desired variation.

If you want consistency, like for judicial sentencing or factual recall, then you average many judgments, or apply rules and standards to the process. However, if you want lots of different views, such as would be important in a creative process, then some variation is a feature, not a concern. Averaging artist work just makes it all mediocre.

Desired variability is one of the big reasons why removing unwanted biases from GenAI isn't trivial. The downside of AI creativity is that it sometimes produces weird or problematic outputs. If that's because of randomness, then the best that can be done is post-AI content filters, which will usually not please everyone. If we decrease weirdness at its root, then we might get a less creative AI. That will sometimes be desirable, but it should be a use-dependent choice.

Reducing Math Bias

Averaging does nothing for bias though, as shown in Figure 13. It decreases the spread of the judgments but doesn't affect the average error—the bias—one iota.

Averaging judgments can even bake in bias. Imagine three of four asylum judges agreeing on a sentence. Taking the majority answer will reduce the impact of the outlier, but if the disagreeing judge was the ethically unbiased one, then you surely don't want to reduce their influence.

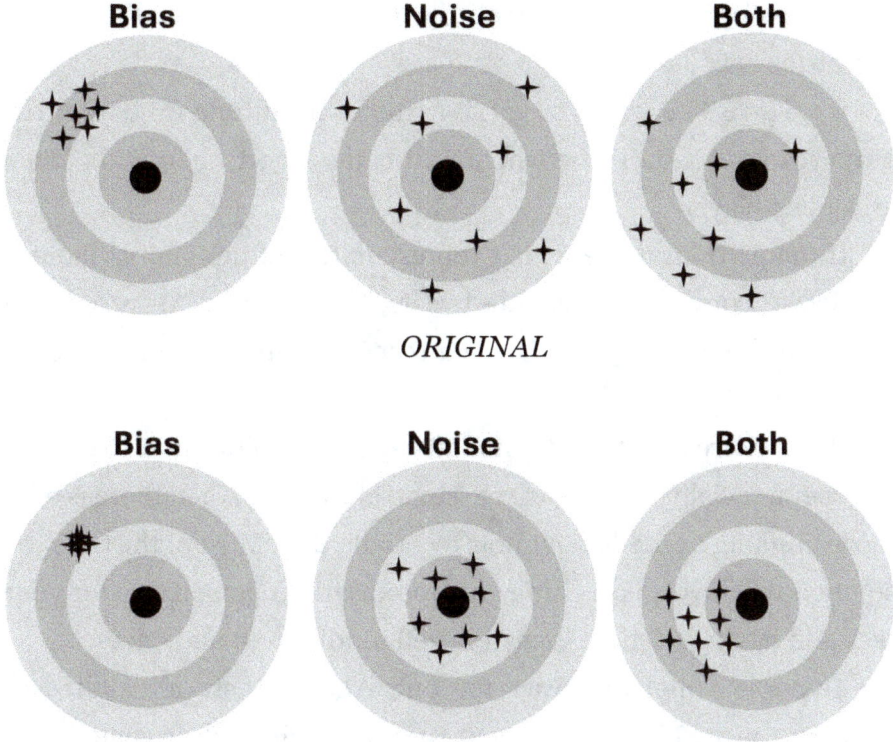

ORIGINAL

NOISE REDUCED BY HALF

Figure 13. Illustration of the effect of averaging on bias and noise.

Reducing bias is inherently more complicated than reducing noise. You need to know the target, and people disagree much of the time on what that should be. Without clearly defining the desired AI behavior, we can't be sure there is math bias.

Back in 2015 it was on the AI engineers to fix the photo labeling issue. Users didn't have any control. We still talk about bias as if it's all on the AI companies to fix.

Yet with AI we have responsibility too. We are AI developers when we use AI. We are now the geeks, but we no longer must speak geek-ese. Within each AI conversation, we are injecting information into AI that modifies the way it behaves. We are engineering a custom AI. It's our job to specify the target for that AI offspring. Much of the time a good prompt is sufficient to overcome an AI model's generic, out-of-the-box nature.

If we give AI a vague target, it assumes it's hitting it—even if the output is nonsense. If the whole wall is the target, then yeah, I'm a great dart player.

If the AI training data isn't representative of humanity, like if it learned to converse by reading tweets, then there is AI-introduced bias, and the AI companies have a responsibility to identify and fix those distortions.

If it is representative of humanity and we don't want it to be, like if it spews racially biased garbage some of the time, then there is a lot more thinking needed about how to handle that. Most of the time the solution will involve choosing an appropriate AI personality for your task and having AI models customized for different audiences.

There is simply no way for one AI to satisfy all audiences simultaneously. If I'm teaching about recognizing subtle gender bias in prose, I might want to have AI create several passages with such biases intentionally inserted. I have an ethical use for an unethical AI behavior.

Even if we deal with AI's bias, there are the ethical and psychological biases we have that can mean we ignore unbiased AI output that's different from what we expect or desire. People can be more biased than AI and can introduce bias in using an AI.

Like I said, bias is more complicated.

The conversation about AI bias often does not feel constructive to me. It's one of the first things educators want students to know about, but the way it's described it feels like warning without remedy. The vibe is that it's up to the AI companies to fix, or that it's an inherent property of AI methods.

The reality is more complicated.

Any categorization, regression, ranking, or pattern transformation essentially imposes a biased interpretation of the input data. Math bias is necessary; it's the unwanted biases we need to avoid.

Sometimes AI is less biased than people. Sometimes people insert bias by using AI inappropriately. And sometimes ethical bias isn't really math bias. It's noise.

We reduce unwanted bias when we can better pin down the intended targets in the form of our prompts and additional documentation that we provide.

AI engineers can reduce some forms of bias by training AI on higher quality, more varied and voluminous, and less biased data, and by carefully training the AI to minimize model defects.

Right now, some biases aren't easy to overcome. WEIRD (Western, Educated, Industrialized, Rich, and Democratic) bias[200] is a known concern in AI, reflecting the predominance of certain perspectives in training data. AI research is increasingly addressing this bias by incorporating diverse, multilingual, and culturally representative datasets, but some challenges are unavoidable. Lower prevalence of data from minority perspectives means the AI will likely perform worse in that context than a WEIRD context.

ERROR ANALYSIS

Measuring the performance level of AI on various complex tasks is a hard problem, one that increasingly must rely on hand-crafted challenges that are intended to be difficult.

AI performance analysis has dramatically transformed as AI has gotten more sophisticated.[201] What began as relatively straightforward evaluations of accuracy and fluency has evolved into assessment methodologies that must account for nuanced capabilities like reasoning, creativity, and ethical judgment. Traditional metrics have been supplemented by more sophisticated evaluation frameworks that examine models' abilities to maintain consistent reasoning across long contexts, detect and avoid harmful outputs, and demonstrate understanding rather than shallow pattern matching. This evolution reflects the fundamental challenge that as AI systems become more capable, our methods for measuring and understanding their performance must become correspondingly more sophisticated.

Some of the modern AI evaluations are complicated and specialized, but there's one error analysis for classifications (from AI or people) that's a great introduction to the error analysis subject and super useful. Many tasks that we give AI are classification tasks, where it's trained to decide whether something fits within one or more exclusive categories. A table called a *confusion matrix* is used to analyze classification errors.

Let's start with a binary classification. Imagine a medical device is being tested on its ability to correctly diagnose cancer. There are four possibilities: a correct positive diagnosis, a correct negative one, a false positive, or a false negative. The number of diagnoses in each of those categories can be shown in a confusion matrix as in Table 1.

Table 1. Confusion matrix for a binary classification challenge. Each quadrant contains a count of the number of test examples fitting that cell.

		AI Answer	
		Cancer	**No Cancer**
Truth	**Cancer**	True Positive (TP)	False Positive (FP)
	No Cancer	False Negative (FN)	True Negative (TN)

A different confusion matrix exists for each point on the ROC curve described in Chapter 2.

From this simple table, a variety of metrics can be generated. A partial list is:

- *What fraction of the AI-declared cancers were correct?*
  Positive Predictive Value (PPV) [a.k.a. precision] = TP/(TP+FP)

- *What fraction of the true cancers did AI detect?*
  Probability of Detection (PD) [a.k.a. recall, sensitivity, or hit rate]
  PD = TP/(TP+FN)

- *What fraction of non-cancers did AI say were cancerous?*
  Probability of False Detection (PFD) = FP/(FP+TN)

- *What fraction of AI's non-cancer declarations are correct?*

  Negative Predictive Value (NPV)=TN/(FN+TN)

The importance of the metrics is application dependent. In medical diagnostics, a false negative (missing a disease) might have very different consequences than a false positive (diagnosing a disease that isn't present). Incorrectly marking important emails as spam (false positive) is generally worse than letting a few spam emails through (false negative). The implications of falsely convicting an innocent person versus letting a guilty person go free are profoundly different.

In many cases, the acceptable error rate or the preferred characteristics of the classification are based on the consequences of the judgment. If there's an additional human review after the AI makes a classification, then a higher false positive rate might be tolerable, but a low false negative rate is desired. The human will want to know not many cancers were missed if the AI is doing the initial screening. That doesn't mean the human review makes the judgment better. In a 2024 study of medical diagnosis, AI performed better on its own then either solo doctors or doctors with the AI.[202] The humans overruled the more accurate AI.

Confusion matrices can also be used for many-class challenges. A hypothetical one is in Table 2. Each row represents the actual category, and each column represents the AI-decided category. The diagonal represents correct categorizations, while off-diagonal elements show various types of misclassifications.

Table 2. Hypothetical confusion matrix for a four-category challenge

		AI Answer			
		A	**B**	**C**	**D**
Truth	**A**	50	1	5	5
	B	2	35	12	5
	C	4	20	40	6
	D	1	0	2	7

For AI classification systems, confusion matrices are invaluable for fine-tuning performance. They help developers understand not just the overall accuracy, but the specific types of errors being made.

Confusion matrices can be used to illustrate several key ideas:

- *Bias:* In Table 2, categories B and C are more often confused with one another than other categories (i.e. the off-diagonal B/C comparisons have larger numbers). When the AI says it's category B (second column), its errors are skewed toward category C. That might be because those categories are more difficult to distinguish, but if that categorization bias is ethically troublesome, then confusion matrices are the first step in determining whether there's a problem.

- *Cost-Sensitive Learning:* Not all errors are equal. Just as humans weigh the consequences of different types of mistakes, AI systems can be tuned to prioritize avoiding certain types of errors. If one category is dark-skinned human faces, and another is gorilla faces, then misclassifications of human faces as gorillas should have a much higher cost than other errors. While the cost of errors is a human question, the confusion matrix provides the raw material for such valuations.

- *Prevalence and Base Rates:* A high accuracy can be misleading if one class is much more common than others. This relates to the human cognitive bias of neglecting base rates in probability judgments. In the table above, true category D occurs much less often than the other categories, so there should be less trust that the statistics related to that category are accurate.

In education, confusion matrices can be applied to a wide range of subjects. Any time you're discussing a concept, there is a binary categorization to potentially discuss—what is "in" the concept, and what is "out."

I don't have to tell educators that assessment can be a complex topic. Confusion matrices are only for the classification decision niche, but that relates to so much of the statistics people get in life.

BIAS IS NICHE SPECIFIC

When AI provides inconsistent answers to similar questions, it often signals we're in territory where its concept characterizations are uncertain. When responses mix clearly accurate information with subtle errors, it might indicate we're at the edges of its knowledge domains.

Your best friend in AI interaction is wisdom that anticipates what can go wrong and steers the AI to stifle its worst instincts. AI can appear biased or unbiased, accurate or inaccurate, depending a great deal on the conversational context you establish.

For instance, if you task an AI with helping to plan a lesson about societal bias and discrimination, I do not expect it to express overtly biased viewpoints. Information about educating on bias is largely academic; general opinions on bias are not. The educational context makes a huge difference.

Medical discussions, for example, likely draw from legitimate, voluminous academic and professional data sources that emphasize reducing bias, improving cultural sensitivity, and providing evidence-based information. That's especially true if the niche you define through your prompting emphasizes legit medical information over rumor (e.g., you request output using medical terminology). If you're an educator, and further narrow the niche to medical education, then the training data fodder for that realm is unlikely to use prejudicial language. Though the medical system itself may have biases, the information sources discussing medical education typically strive to avoid perpetuating them.

To be clear, defining the AI's niche well is no guarantee that all biases will go away. It might introduce other biases particular to that niche or include cross-cutting biases that many niches share. Medical literature isn't likely to be overtly discriminatory, but studies are more prevalent for certain demographics. If you're using AI to generate medical education case studies, you'd better tell it to design cases with patient diversity in mind.

The point is only that the biases and inaccuracies in the niche are the ones that matter, not all biases and inaccuracies. For that reason, I pay more attention to the AI's general performance level in a domain than to highly publicized biases and errors.

***

Some educators won't open the cover on AI because they've heard so much about its inaccuracies and biases that they just don't see the point. That may have been reinforced by a few uses where the AI clearly didn't provide what was needed.

I'm not here to say you should ignore AI errors, but as with other aspects of this book I'm asking that you take a more nuanced perspective. Yes, AI hallucinates and has biases. But it also helps us catch our own mistakes, offers fresh perspectives, and processes information in ways that often complement human thinking. The key is learning how to use it wisely—not expecting perfection.

It's not like interacting with humans is error free. We're often listening to people spout nonsense. We have biases. We misremember facts. We jump to conclusions. We're inconsistent in our judgments.

Yet we've developed ways to work around these limitations. We should fact-check important information. We should seek second opinions. We should use structured processes for critical decisions.

AI makes different errors than people, including stuff we find simple. It also does stuff we find impossible. The key is to use human and AI strengths appropriately.

There are three aspects of this chapter that are most important:

1. *We're not helpless to baked-in error from AI company choices.* Good prompting, including more example data, can fix a lot of error, excessive generality, and irrelevance.

2. *Reducing AI error is helped by metaknowledge about error.* At a minimum, we need common grounding to avoid talking past one another.

3. *There's no magical prompt; dealing with AI requires wisdom, as with people.* Teachers notice subtle cues from students that signal potential confusion. Similarly, working effectively with AI requires developing sensitivity to its behavioral patterns. You're going to get wisdom from experience with AI, not presentation slides.

Yes, AI hallucinates and is biased. And what are we going to do about it?

KEY META-PRINCIPLES

- **Recognizing and Fixing Errors:** Identifying different kinds of AI errors (e.g., bias, hallucinations, noise) and understanding strategies to address them.

- **Acceptable Error Levels:** Evaluating what levels of error are tolerable depending on the task, context, and stakes.

- **Errors as Learning Opportunities:** Viewing errors as opportunities for refinement and improvement in both AI and human systems.

- **AI Performance Analysis:** Analyzing AI performance through error patterns to diagnose issues and improve system design.

EXAMPLE LEARNING PROGRESSION

K-5	• Recognize simple mistakes and discuss how they can lead to improvement. • Explore the idea of acceptable levels of error in everyday tasks. • Practice identifying patterns in repeated mistakes.
6-8	• Categorize different types of errors in familiar contexts. • Discuss how different tasks require different levels of performance. • Experiment with iterative improvement by analyzing patterns in mistakes.
9-12	• Identify and analyze AI-specific errors (e.g., hallucinations, bias, or misclassification) using simple models or AI tools. • Explore real-world examples to evaluate acceptable error levels in high- versus low-stakes contexts. • Develop strategies to analyze and correct errors systematically.
College	• Design and evaluate AI systems with a focus on error analysis, testing how different conditions (e.g., biased data or noisy inputs) affect outcomes. • Debate acceptable error metrics and thresholds in professional applications, incorporating ethical and societal considerations. • Build projects or models that iteratively improve performance by identifying and addressing specific error patterns.

10.

GETTING STARTED

S ome of my best educational experiences were in co-learning environments, where the teacher was learning along with the student. In the Prologue I mentioned my first computer programming class in high school in the early 1980s. That teacher was just learning to code. In college I had a coding class with an unusual language that we got as a beta version. The teacher knew coding better than any of the students, but we also had to debug the way the language executed. We addressed those problems together.

There's a notion that teachers must be experts before introducing new topics or technologies to their students. While doctors constantly incorporate new treatments they're still learning about, and engineers regularly tackle unfamiliar problems, many educators mistakenly feel they need complete mastery before bringing something into their classroom.

This mindset, though well-intentioned, creates several problems. It drastically limits instruction, particularly in emerging technologies and complex challenges. It can delay important learning opportunities as teachers wait for enough expertise. Perhaps most damagingly, it reinforces a model of education where students are passive recipients of knowledge rather than active participants in discovery.

The most powerful learning occurs when tackling challenges without clear answers. When students have genuine agency in their learning—when they're truly discovering rather than just absorbing— they develop deeper understanding and stronger engagement. This is especially true for conceptual learning about complex, nuanced topics where expertise comes through experience and reflection rather than memorization.

The maker movement of the 2010s was an instructive example of what's possible with student and teacher co-learning. That paradigm encourages a hands-on, project-based approach to learning. Students actively engage in designing, building, and creating using a variety of tools and technologies.

When 3D printers first entered schools, teachers had no prior experience with the technology. A training deficit often accompanies the introduction of new technologies. However, delaying instruction until teachers are fully trained ultimately disadvantages students. By the time educators master a rapidly evolving technology, it may already be obsolete.

Maker tools are highly versatile, constrained primarily by imagination. Some teachers positioned themselves as co-learners, guiding the overall experience while being open to discoveries and insights from their students.

The results were often wonderful.[203] Students, unburdened by preconceptions about how things "should" work, would try approaches their teachers hadn't considered. They'd discover novel solutions to design problems or innovative ways to troubleshoot 3D printer issues. Teachers who embraced this dynamic found their classrooms transformed into genuine learning communities where everyone was growing and discovering at once.

This wasn't just about technology; these classrooms fostered deeper understanding of design thinking, problem-solving, and iterative innovation. The specific technical skills were almost secondary to these deeper principles that emerged through shared exploration.

AI education is at a similar crossroads. The technology is evolving rapidly, its implications are vast, and waiting for full understanding before teaching it is counterproductive.

In many schools, the issues of student AI safety and tool management are still not worked out and teaching with AI can be difficult for teachers to manage with all but small groups. But that shouldn't stop schools and educators. As this book has indicated, there's a lot of good stuff to teach without computers that can start with an "oh, by the way" for your current lessons. As for needing to get training before starting, remember that students aren't waiting for training before they start. That could lead to bad habits and unsafe experiences.

Co-learning isn't just necessary in most current situations—it should be preferred. One of my favorite things to do with young children is to feign ignorance about something they know. It always brings a smile. They love teaching! Co-learning, whether with the teacher or other students, can turn a dry, one-way knowledge data pipe into a dynamic, innovative space.

The meta-principles of AI and cognitive systems are too crucial to delay and too valuable to reduce to rote instruction.

This chapter explores how to begin this journey. I'll outline the important ingredients for teaching these concepts and mindsets, look at different implementation approaches, and discuss how to assess understanding in this more fluid learning environment. I hope this is seen as the beginning of a thought process, rather than a prescription. The key is to start where you are, with what you have, rather than waiting for perfect understanding. The modeling of lifelong learning should also not be ignored. When students see ignorance not as a defect but an opportunity to learn, or adults who remain curious about the world, that rubs off.

The paradigm shifts in this book aren't concepts that can simply be memorized or understood through a few lessons. Like any deep shift in thinking, they must be built up through experience, reflection, and gradual insight.

INGREDIENTS FOR TEACHING META-PRINCIPLES

I have been somewhat vocal about the holes in education research regarding the learning of cross-cutting durable skills. Most of learning science has measured learning success by the ability to regurgitate knowledge. Pedagogical experiments are often small, focus on highly quantifiable, short-term metrics, and are as complex as psychological experiments for which replication has been an issue.[204,205,206] This is not to disparage educational researchers; there is a dearth of funding to do larger-scale experiments, and journals and colleges usually encourage novel work, not research replication.

The question of how AI meta-principles are best taught, understanding that such mentalities take years to develop, is yet unclear. Ditto for durable qualities such as creativity, communication, critical thinking, etc.

What we have are clues. Research has exposed some key ingredients of the learning environment for abstract, intuitive skill development.

Here's my list of ingredients for teaching meta-principles.

Complex, Open-Ended Challenges

The foundation for learning meta-principles is engaging with challenges that reveal deeper truths. Concepts related to AI can be taught directly. There can be units on how to analyze AI errors or distributed systems, for example. But really understanding these concepts is not only about how to apply the ideas in a specific context but also about what contexts the notion helps. Both of those skills get engaged when the challenge posed is complex and has many different answers.

Let's say the complex, open-ended challenge is for older students to design an adaptive AI tutoring system for younger students on a particular topic. That's a topic that pulls in both AI and human teaching considerations.

This isn't a straightforward engineering task. Students must grapple with fundamental questions: How do we know if someone understands something? How do different examples affect learning? When should instruction adapt? What feedback helps versus hinders? These questions naturally lead students to discover key principles about both human and artificial intelligence.

Some students might focus on how to represent knowledge at different levels of understanding. Others could explore how to transform complex ideas into simpler ones. Still others might investigate how to recognize when a learner is confused. Through this process, students encounter multiple meta-principles: how patterns emerge from simple interactions, how concepts get transformed between different representations, and how learning systems need to balance exploration with exploitation.

The challenge's complexity creates natural opportunities to compare human and artificial approaches. Students might realize that both students and AI systems need varied examples to develop robust understanding. They could see how both teachers and an AI used for teaching must transform information based on the learner's current understanding.

These insights directly inform AI interaction. The principles behind effective teaching—context, examples, and information transformation—mirror those in AI prompting. Whether or not students ever use AI for assignments, they're developing deeper intuition about how intelligence processes information.

The open-ended nature prevents students from finding ready-made answers while ensuring discoveries feel genuine. As students progress, they can tackle increasingly sophisticated aspects of the challenge, from basic content adaptation to handling misconceptions to developing more personalized learning paths.

It's very unlikely that such intuitions will arise through narrowly scoped activities and projects. While complexity and ambiguity must be presented appropriately for the student age, the notion that we educate from the bottom-up, building knowledge bricks with the hope that someday the accumulated wall will allow big picture insight, just doesn't fit what's needed for abstract conceptual learning. That learning must be instigated from the top-down. In *Wisdom Factories* I called it upside-down learning. It's still about learning from what you practice, but to learn abstract concepts you have to practice making decisions on problems that require them.

Student Agency

This one I already teed up in the discussion of student-teacher co-learning at the beginning of the chapter.

I'll continue with the tutoring system design challenge as an example. While designing an adaptive tutoring system provides a rich context for exploring meta-principles, students might be more curious about other similar challenges. Some may prefer studying animal learning, urban adaptation, or information flow in social networks. The core meta-principles about pattern analysis, adaptation, and information transformation appear in all these systems.

Research shows that when students have genuine choice in their learning context, they show greater persistence with challenging material and develop deeper conceptual understanding.[207] A student fascinated by animal behavior might discover fundamental principles about learning and adaptation by exploring how pets recognize patterns in human behavior and adjust their responses. Another student might uncover similar principles by analyzing how cities transform as populations grow and needs change.

This flexibility in choosing application domains enhances the learning of meta-principles. When students later compare their discoveries across different domains, they begin to see the universality of these principles. The student who studied pet learning might recognize similar patterns in how AI systems learn from feedback. The student who analyzed city development might see parallels in how neural networks adapt to new information.

The chosen domain must offer sufficient complexity and opportunity for discovery. Students need challenges that require thinking—not simply recall—to explore how intelligence processes information. The teacher's role shifts from content delivery to guiding students toward deeper principles in their chosen context.

Learning Through Experience and Productive Struggle

The journey through these challenges must begin with direct experience, not explanation. Research shows that when students encounter concepts through hands-on exploration before formal instruction, they develop more flexible and transferable understanding.[208]

This can seem counterintuitive. Surely explaining the principles first would make the learning more efficient? But efficiency isn't the goal; deep conceptual understanding is.

Consider students exploring how to develop their adaptive tutoring system. Rather than first teaching them about learning theory or information processing, let them begin by trying to teach something simple to each other or to younger students. Their initial attempts will likely be imperfect. Some might rely too heavily on repetition. Others might not recognize when their pupil is confused. They might struggle to adjust their explanations when their first approach fails.

These struggles, what learning scientists call "productive failure," create fertile ground for insight.[209] When students encounter the limitations of their initial approaches, they develop genuine curiosity about better methods. A student who can't tell if their learner truly understands can become primed to explore different ways of recognizing understanding. One whose explanations consistently fail to connect discovers the need for multiple representations of knowledge.

The experience of struggling to recognize and adapt to a learner's needs creates natural parallels to AI systems. Students discover firsthand why both human and AI tutors need varied feedback signals, how they must transform information based on the learner's current understanding, and when they need to try fundamentally different approaches. Because they emerge from direct experience, the insights feel more authentic, and they tend to be more memorable and applicable than if they had simply been explained.[210]

This approach requires teachers to resist the urge to front-load information or correct early misconceptions too quickly. The goal isn't to prevent mistakes but to create space for productive ones that reveal important principles about how learning and intelligence work. Delivering information too early can rob students of the realizations that are critical for mental model changes.[211] When students later encounter formal theories about learning, metacognition, or AI, they have rich personal experiences to connect these ideas to.

The process mirrors how AI neural networks learn through repeated interaction with examples rather than through explicit rules. AI systems develop their capabilities through experience rather than programming, and students develop deeper understanding of meta-principles through direct engagement rather than explanation.

Building Understanding Across Domains

Once students have deeply explored meta-principles in one context, the next crucial step is encountering these same principles in different domains. The goal is to stretch and refine their conceptual understanding.

Research shows that seeing the same principles in varied contexts is crucial for developing flexible, transferable knowledge.[212] More importantly, this cross-domain exploration helps students distinguish fundamental principles from domain-specific details. The student who first explored adaptive tutoring begins to see that certain patterns, like the balance between exploration and exploitation or the need for varied feedback, appear regardless of the specific context.

As discussed in Chapter 4, concept stretching means pushing the boundaries of what students think they understand. A student who grasped how an adaptive tutor needs diverse examples might be challenged to consider how this same principle appears in evolution, where genetic diversity helps species adapt to changing environments. Or they might explore how their insights about feedback in teaching parallel how AI language models learn from human preferences.

This cross-domain exploration naturally leads to richer understanding of AI itself. When students recognize how their own learning depends on varied examples and clear feedback, they intuitively grasp why AI systems need similar ingredients. When they see how their teaching strategies must adapt to different learners, they understand why AI needs different prompting approaches for different tasks.

Reflection and Refinement

Deep understanding of meta-principles requires more than just experiencing them in different contexts. Students need structured opportunities to process these experiences, recognize patterns across them, and refine their approaches. Reflection and refinement need to be woven throughout the learning process.

Research on metacognition shows that the simple act of articulating what we're learning significantly deepens our understanding.[213] But reflection in this context goes beyond just thinking about what we've learned. It involves actively comparing approaches across domains, identifying common principles, and using those insights to improve future attempts.

Consider a student who has explored adaptive systems through both tutoring and city planning. Their reflection might start with surface similarities, such as that both systems need to respond to changing needs. But deeper reflection reveals more fundamental patterns: how feedback loops operate, how systems balance competing demands, or how information gets transformed between different representations. These insights can then fuel refinement of their original approaches.

This shift from learner to teacher creates powerful opportunities for understanding. When students design learning experiences that include meta-principle consideration, they must decide what examples will best reveal key patterns, how to structure productive failure, and when to encourage cross-domain connections. While a later stage in a learning progression, this meta-teaching experience deepens their grasp of the principles while developing crucial skills in communication and knowledge transfer.

A tinkering attitude plays a crucial role in this refinement process. Complex challenges, including some interactions with AI, aren't solved in one swoop and may never be truly solved. They need to be approached through systematic experimentation.

Bringing It Together

The kind of pedagogy I've described isn't unexplored, but it represents a significant shift from traditional education. It prioritizes deep understanding of meta-principles over rapid content coverage. This inevitably means some tradeoffs.

The most obvious is time. When students explore challenges deeply enough to discover fundamental principles, they cover less material than in traditional instruction. You can't simultaneously optimize for coverage and discovery. But students who understand these meta-principles develop stronger capabilities for tackling novel problems and learning new content quickly.[214] And they might actually remember the lessons over the long term.

Perhaps more importantly, this approach might transform student engagement. When challenges are genuinely complex, allow personal choice in exploration, and connect to real principles about how intelligence works, students might surprise themselves with their level of investment. A student who normally rushes through homework might spend hours refining their adaptive tutoring system design, not because they have to, but because they're genuinely curious about making it work better.

There will be some students who will struggle with the openness of the challenges, and others might miss the structure of traditional instruction. But even these struggles become learning opportunities. The need for detailed knowledge doesn't go away. It's just transformed into a knowledge-on-demand paradigm. Understanding when different approaches work best, for both humans and AI, is itself a crucial meta-principle.

The same patterns that make this approach effective for students—the need for varied examples, the value of productive failure, the importance of cross-domain connections—apply equally to teachers implementing it. Start with one challenge in one subject area. Allow students to uncover key principles. Then gradually expand to other domains and more complex challenges. The progression itself embodies the meta-principles it aims to teach.

Success shouldn't be about fact recall or individual challenge performance. Instead, look for growing sophistication in how students approach novel problems, their ability to recognize familiar patterns in new contexts, and their capacity to adapt strategies based on experience. These capabilities serve students well whether they're working with AI, advancing in their studies, or tackling real-world challenges.

CUSTOMIZATION EXAMPLES

There are several ways that educators might begin implementing these meta-principles, from integrating them into existing units, developing dedicated units or courses, or reimagining broader curriculum frameworks.

For fitting existing units or developing new ones, I'll show how AI can help brainstorm the customization. This is the beginning of a customization conversation, but depending on the complexity of the change, AI can also help create lesson and assignment materials and assessments. Don't take these initial AI responses to be output that I agree with. It's a starting point, but one that saves a ton of time.

Adding to Existing Units

AI Prompt (a ChatGPT-4o rephrasing of my prompt on 1/12/25)
[Teacher uploads *AI Wisdom Volume 1* into the AI.]
"I'm a 10th grade ELA teacher in the U.S. who is teaching a unit (12 lessons, 50-minutes each) on poetry. By the end of this unit, students will be able to:

- Analyze how specific poetic devices (imagery, metaphor, sound, form) create meaning, developed through close reading of Frost, Shakespeare, Brooks, and Angelou

- Create and revise original poetry that deliberately employs these devices for effect, developed through guided practice and workshop sessions
- Articulate poetry's relevance to their own experience through both analytical discussion and creative expression, developed through class discussions and final presentations

Most lessons are currently organized to either analyze one poem or for students to write and present their poems. A quarter of my students struggle with reading. I need to keep three major graded assignments and still cover the required poetry content. The students have already learned about literary devices and historical context of romantic and modernist poetry. They do well with creative projects but struggle with abstract analysis.

How could meta-principles from the book be included in the poetry unit? Output a concise list of possibilities."

ChatGPT-4o response (2/11/2025)

"Here are some ways you could incorporate meta-principles from *AI Wisdom* into your poetry unit:

1. *Pattern Analyzing* – Guide students to see poetry as a pattern-recognition exercise, where form, rhyme, and rhythm function like networks of meaning rather than isolated rules.
2. *Transforming* – Teach poetry as a transformation of experience into language, exploring how metaphors and imagery shift perception (similar to AI's transformation of data into insights).
3. *Knowing* – Discuss how poetry conveys meaning differently from prose, paralleling how AI and humans "know" differently (AI statistically, humans conceptually and emotionally).

4. *Creative Constraints* – Encourage students to experiment with constraints (like sonnets, haikus) to enhance creativity, similar to how AI generates new outputs within structured limits.

5. *Distributed Meaning* – Emphasize that poetry's meaning emerges across words and lines, rather than being tied to single elements—similar to how AI and human memory are distributed.

6. *Error and Refinement* – Use poetry revision to reinforce that creativity is an iterative process, just as AI refines its models through errors and adjustments.

7. *Adaptive Interpretation* – Show how poems change in meaning depending on context and reader interpretation, mirroring how AI adapts to different inputs and interactions.

8. *Analogies and AI Intuition* – Have students create analogies for poetic devices, reinforcing *AI Wisdom's* argument that understanding intelligence involves conceptual abstraction.

9. *Cognitive Bias and Language* – Explore how poetic devices shape perception and emotion, tying into discussions about how AI and humans interpret information differently.

10. *Complex, Open-Ended Challenges* – Instead of single-answer analysis, structure discussions as explorations of multiple interpretations, mirroring AI's handling of ambiguous data.

11. *Student Agency in Meaning-Making* – Connect poetry to students' personal experiences, as *AI Wisdom* suggests learning is strongest when individuals shape their understanding.

12. *Interdisciplinary Connections* – Relate poetry to AI concepts (e.g., neural networks and rhythm, machine learning and poetic experimentation) to reinforce cross-disciplinary thinking."

Developing Dedicated Units

AI Prompt

[Teacher uploads *AI Wisdom Volume 1* into the AI.]

"I want to include a unit on AI error analysis in the general education math class I teach for first- and second-year undergraduates at our college. Most of the students are nursing, business, and humanities majors, but most haven't taken any courses in their major yet. They will have learned about basic statistical calculations previously in the course. Using AI Wisdom (attached) and assuming a two-week unit for a three-credit hour course, outline the unit, explain the primary forms of experience the students will learn from, and give an example of a homework assignment from that unit. Give a concise overview; don't break it down into specific class periods."

ChatGPT-4o response (2/11/2025)
"*Unit Overview*

This two-week unit introduces students to the concept of AI error analysis, leveraging their foundational statistical knowledge. The focus will be on how AI makes decisions, why errors occur, and how they can be detected, quantified, and mitigated. The unit will bridge AI concepts with real-world applications relevant to students' diverse future professions in nursing, business, and the humanities.

Primary Learning Experiences
Students will engage in:

- *Case-Based Learning* – Analyzing real-world AI decision errors in healthcare (misdiagnoses), finance (biased loan approvals), and journalism (misinformation).
- *Hands-On Data Exploration* – Using spreadsheets or AI to examine datasets where AI has made incorrect predictions.
- *Mathematical Error Metrics* – Applying statistical measures (e.g., accuracy, precision, recall, F1-score) to evaluate AI system performance.
- *AI Testing Simulation* – Manually adjusting AI-generated outputs based on statistical error analysis, discussing factors influencing accuracy.
- *Ethical Implications Discussion* – Exploring the societal impact of AI errors, particularly their consequences in healthcare and financial decision-making.

Sample Homework Assignment

Title: Diagnosing AI Errors in Real-World Cases
Objective: Apply statistical concepts to evaluate AI performance in a real-world scenario.
Instructions:

- Read a short case study on an AI-based diagnostic tool for detecting pneumonia in chest X-rays.
- Given a dataset of 100 cases, where the AI diagnosed 70 cases correctly, misclassified 10 healthy patients as sick, and failed to identify 20 actual pneumonia cases:
- Calculate accuracy, precision, recall, and F1-score.
- Discuss how these metrics reveal different strengths and weaknesses of the AI system.

- Reflect: If you were a healthcare administrator, what changes might you make to improve patient safety based on these results?"

ASSESSING META-PRINCIPLE UNDERSTANDING

Traditional assessment methods, with their emphasis on isolated facts and procedures, aren't well suited for evaluating understanding of meta-principles. When learning goals involve recognizing patterns across domains or developing new ways to transform information, multiple choice tests fall short. Yet we need ways to gauge student progress and guide their development.

The key is focusing assessment on how students handle novel situations. Rather than testing whether they can recite definitions or follow procedures, we want to see how they approach unfamiliar challenges that require similar patterns of thinking. Can they recognize relevant patterns in new contexts? Can they adapt strategies they've used before? Can they articulate why certain approaches might or might not work?

Since traditional assessments fall short in measuring conceptual transfer, alternative approaches such as game-based learning offer promising solutions, whether computerized or not. When students encounter new game scenarios that embed familiar meta-principles, their responses reveal their level of understanding. Research shows that game-based assessment can effectively measure higher-order thinking skills.[215] The key is designing scenarios that require applying meta-principles in novel ways. These days AI can be a huge accelerant to game development. Even if a teacher doesn't get the game design completely right (e.g., there's a way to get a high score but avoid realizing the meta-principles), involving students in the debugging and game design adaptation are also instructive.

Consider an assessment where students must figure out how an unfamiliar system works. Maybe it's a new game with hidden rules, or a simulated ecosystem with unknown relationships. Rather than testing specific knowledge, evaluate their approach. What patterns do they look for? How do they test their hypotheses? When do they shift strategies? How do they use what they've learned in one part of the system to understand others?

The quality of student questions becomes another important metric. As students develop deeper understanding of meta-principles, their questions tend to become more sophisticated. They move from surface-level "what" questions to deeper "how" and "why" questions. They start asking about patterns and relationships rather than just facts. This progression in inquiry sophistication provides valuable insight into their developing understanding.

Project documentation offers another window into student thinking. The focus shouldn't exclusively be on the solution the student devised, but on evidence of meta-principle understanding.

The emphasis should be on developing robust, transferable understanding rather than memorizing specific procedures or facts. Let them look up the formula for a Positive Predictive Value (PPV) error metric, but make sure they understand in what situations PPV is an appropriate metric, when the calculation is more uncertain, and how the statistic can be used in misleading ways.

***

As I said at the beginning of the book, I'm laying out a backdrop. I don't have all the answers on the best ways to integrate these topics into existing curricula or the best way for students to learn the concepts. That's the nature of something new. The key is to try, learn, and quickly iterate. In the spirit of co-learning, let the students in on the uncertainty. Have them comment on the unit, assignment, or exercise and what might be done better next time.

One key ingredient remains unmentioned. The meta-principles being taught can be applied to any realm, but students do need to understand the principles' relationship to AI. You can teach a lot of this stuff without mentioning AI, but then students don't get the key connection I'm hoping you'll create.

When the world is changing rapidly and you're developing anything that is intended to affect human minds, then the appropriate strategy isn't to think for months and years about how to do it best. In software development, such uncertainties led to the development of a process called Agile, where goals and tactics are adjusted regularly.[216] Its use has resulted in a much higher software development project success rate, and its orientation toward learning by doing are equally applicable to curriculum and learning environment design regarding AI.

11.

WHAT'S NEXT?

T he chorus started pretty quickly following the release of GPT-4 in the Spring of 2023. The base method behind AI LLMs (the *transformer model*) has fundamental limits, many said. ChatGPT-4 required a neural net and training dataset many times larger than that of ChatGPT-3.5, and the prediction of how much better AI would perform as scale increased faced a fundamental problem. It would take oodles more training data, computational power, and AI neural net connections for transformer models to get much better. Since it had taken billions of dollars to build GPT-4, the logic was that future advances would be smaller than the jump from GPT-3.5 to GPT-4.

There is real science behind this view; the transformer model method does have limits.[217] But many have taken this much farther than a limit to a specific method. They prophesize that AI as a business won't be profitable and won't have the resources to improve. That AI will never go superhuman because of these limitations.

I always thought that was laughable. It's wishful thinking from those who don't wish further AI advance and have decided the way to deal with that is to latch onto whatever theory of AI limitation comes along. To be clear, I don't wish AI to advance more at all, but it will … a lot. The question is how we deal with it, and I think those expressing AI's upcoming downfall are misleading people.

This skepticism about AI's limits isn't new—history is full of examples where technological progress defied expectations.

PREDICTING AI'S FUTURE

There have always been numerous ways for AI to improve. Most are unexplored. Since innovations can't be precisely predicted, it's easy to point to current limits. But the better way to analyze rapidly improving and youthful realms isn't to latch onto current limits, but to examine the historical ability for the field to overcome prior limits.

The easiest example is Moore's law. In undergraduate studies in the 1980s I had a couple of classes in semiconductor design. One of my professors was clear that we were approaching physical size limits of transistors very soon, and that computers wouldn't keep getting smaller. He was wrong, and demonstrably so within about a decade.

Transistors kept shrinking, and innovations in design and organization made chips increasingly powerful. Moore's law was originally a prediction of the pace of improvement in transistor density but has been recast to describe computational improvement more generally. Under that framing, Moore's Law has driven a hundred-million-fold increase in instructions per second over the past five decades.[218] That's true even though at each stage the end of Moore's law was being predicted (and still is). It's not a law after all; it's just a strong empirical trend.

The history of innovation is a more reliable predictor than the limits of existing technology.

Predictions of AI improvement have been overconservative for at least the past decade. In 2017, a survey of 352 AI researchers predicted that AI would be able to write solid high school essays by 2026.[219] It happened in a bit more than half the predicted time. (By the way, was the education system paying attention in 2017? Because AI researchers could have told them change was coming!)

AI researchers couldn't look beyond the horizon. They were being asked to make predictions about when innovation could happen. Most of the time that means we give things a ten-to-twenty-year prediction—the general forecasting answer when some kind of invention is needed along the way.

That's different now. Superhuman cognitive AI is within the horizon now. In many respects, AI is already superhuman when compared to the average person on many tasks.

This fast-moving AI train isn't slowing down. It's speeding up. In December 2024, as I write this, OpenAI has announced the upcoming release of its o3 model. It scored 87.7% on a test designed by researchers to evaluate complex reasoning, surpassing the human average of 85%. The prior ChatGPT model, o1, scored only in the range of 7%, depending on the version. But o1 was released only weeks beforehand. Oh, and o3 also scored as the (gulp) 175th best competitive coder in the world.[220] Yikes!

AI can advance through at least four pathways:

- *Better neural nets or underlying pattern analyzing "chip."* For example, the o3 neural net includes layers that integrate knowledge graphs.
- *Iterative "reflection."* This is done either through having the same model do additional passes on its own output, or by having another AI instance that critiques or influences the way the problem is being approached.
- *Combinations of AI systems,* either multiple in one product, teams of AI models, or larger scale AI "societies." DeepSeek exploited this avenue by using a "mixture-of-experts" model instead of one general-purpose model.[221]
- *Agents* that act, not just muse.

In Volume 1 I've only highlighted the neural network base of modern AI, the "chip" that's the first improvement path. The other forms of AI improvement will be discussed in Volume 2.

For now, just realize that AI isn't going to stop advancing. It's reasonable to assume that quite soon AI will be able to do anything on a computer that a person can do. That means it could do any assignment. It could pretend to be any person. It could be set up to deceive. If you're imagining today's AI, and only today's AI, then you're not thinking even months ahead. You're not understanding how big a deal AI is.

VOLUME 2 PREVIEW

Effective managers need two fundamental types of knowledge about their team members. First, they must understand their cognitive style—how each person thinks, learns, and processes information. Second, they need to know how to leverage those individual characteristics toward productive goals. What tasks suit them best? How do I communicate effectively with them? How to integrate their work with others?

This first volume deals with AI's cognitive core. I've described its neural net foundations, its learning mechanisms, its conceptual nature, and its error patterns. This knowledge forms the bedrock for effective AI interaction, just as understanding how team members tick forms the foundation for good management.

Volume 2 turns to the second challenge—how to effectively direct and integrate AI capabilities. While other works focus on the mechanics of prompting or specific tool usage, I'll continue exploring the deeper paradigm shifts and mental models needed to orchestrate

AI effectively. I examine how to think about AI collaboration, team building, and system design. Those need mindsets too, such as treating each AI interaction as a problem-solving process and each safety or ethical choice as a system analysis. It means treating AI as a savant-like servant rather than an equal partner and understanding the most common types of tasks and how AI and human roles can be allocated.

Neither book focuses on mastering today's AI tools, as that knowledge may be obsolete by the time you read this. It's about developing the mental frameworks that will serve you as AI continues to evolve. Just as Volume 1 showed how understanding AI's nature changes how we think about intelligence itself, Volume 2 will show how understanding AI's practical applications changes how we think about work and human potential.

Working with AI, like working with people, requires intuitive skills rooted in wisdom. People need the ability to recognize which approaches will work best for different situations. Just as experienced managers develop a feel for how to handle various team dynamics, students and teachers can learn to recognize patterns in AI interaction that guide better decisions about when and how to use these powerful tools.

Volume 2 points out glaring gaps in educational emphases. Skills of management and leadership are now important for everyone, not just those who will oversee people. Understanding AI teams and collectives involves sociologist and anthropologist skills too. The meta-principles of search, judgment, and other common tasks aren't generally taught. The system analysis emphasis needed for applied safety and ethics decisions is lacking.

The future belongs to those who can effectively orchestrate both human and artificial intelligence. Volume 2 will give you the mental models needed to become that orchestrator.

***

I often start presentations about AI to educators by dealing with two main obstacles to change: emotions and knowledge.

They are connected. Studies consistently show that those trained in AI or are using it regularly develop more nuanced views. That's consistent with my approach. I'm not trying to change minds. I'm trying to inform them and move them toward nuance instead of black and white.

Knowledge about AI can be quite siloed. I relate it to the story about the blind men and the elephant. Each touches a different part of the animal and reports very different stories about what they're observing. Those who use it for coding don't typically write long documents too and getting it to write or brainstorm only reveals aspects of AI's faults and abilities. The less skilled someone is with AI, the less likely they are to receive useful responses.

We know that AI prompting instruction can improve at least the perceived utility of AI. This is analogous to having a bit of knowledge about negotiating tactics. Useful, but not enough to be a good negotiator. Negotiation requires experience, but excelling at it demands a deep understanding of the other party's personality and psychological drivers. You need to anticipate how they might respond and adapt to what you do.

That's what this book is intended to do. I want you to understand what you're dealing with in AI.

Take this in baby steps if giant leaps are too overwhelming. Now you know that AI instruction doesn't necessarily require interacting with AI, though AI use is often important at older ages when challenge complexity increases. You can also teach this stuff by augmenting rather than replacing existing emphases.

AI is a really big deal, and I fear that schools who slow-roll teaching about it will quickly lose relevance in a world infused with it.

Like it or not, AI will be a big part of student lives. Don't worry about perfection. Just get started.

ACKNOWLEDGEMENTS

Writing a book is a journey. I don't start with a well-defined script. This book started as something quite different. Unlike what traditional publishers demand, where a detailed outline and marketing plan is submitted for consideration, I write a lot first and then decide how to organize it. Sure, I generate an outline, but it isn't going to feel right until some of it gets fleshed out, and along the way the outline gets ripped up multiple times and recast.

I self-published because I couldn't tolerate the year-long delay that academic or trade book publishers would impose. I believe I'm writing about timeless AI underpinnings, but some of the narrative about the current context will surely sound dated a year from now.

Besides, this is the critical time. Teachers, districts, colleges, and entire countries are finally beginning to define what AI education will be (or the more limiting "AI literacy" that is usually about learning to prompt and use AI tools). I think they need the bigger picture framing that this book offers, instead of teaching about AI at a surface level or relegating it to STEM instruction.

In the summer of 2024, I started consolidating what I'd previously written down about AI education for the typical student. Then I had several discussions with Pat Yongpradit and Marty Creel at Teach.ai. They exposed me to the urgency of curriculum discussions, the AI literacy framings that had already been generated, and the nature of the debates. They both have a super ability to think at the abstract and multi-factor level that such big changes require.

Though the book has changed a lot in the interim, those discussions were critical to my thinking.

Several great thinkers read and commented on all or part of the alpha version of the book, when Volume 1 and 2 were still under one cover. Those readers included a couple of people from my former career: Richard Danzig (former Secretary of the Navy, consultant to U.S. intelligence and defense agencies, and affiliated with national security policy analysis organizations), and Robert Seater (game and system analysis expert at MIT Lincoln Laboratory). In the education sphere, I got feedback from top notch AI and education thinkers who are surely way too busy to read a draft book but nevertheless did so. I'm grateful to Stefan Bauschard (K-16 debate and AI-in-education leader), Darren Coxon (Kompass Education, former school director and English department lead), Jason Gulya (English Professor at Berkeley College), Jon Ippolito (Professor of New Media and Director of Digital Curation at the University of Maine), Sam Liberty (Northeastern University game design professor and independent gaming consultant), Justin Lai (Educational Technologist, La Pietra – Hawai'i School for Girls), and Emily Rush (Center for Teaching Excellence and Innovation, Rush University) for their thoughtful commentaries.

I thank caffeine, lots of long walks, the fortune to be exposed to so many great thinkers through the years, and the encouragement of friends in education like Mark DeFusco and Laura Gambino.

Thanks go to Bethany Brown at Cadence Publishing and Gwyn Flowers at GKS Creative for their excellent publishing and cover support.

GLOSSARY

This glossary was generated by Claude Sonnet on January 9, 2025. I added a few entries and made small corrections.

Activation Function: A mathematical operation in artificial neurons that helps neural networks recognize non-linear patterns, allowing them to capture complex relationships in data.

(Artificial) Neural Network (or Neural Net): A system of connected artificial neurons that work together to recognize patterns, inspired by how brain cells connect and communicate.

Alignment: The degree to which AI behavior matches human intentions and values.

Bias (Mathematical): The tendency for an AI system to consistently deviate from desired outputs in a particular direction, distinct from social or ethical bias.

Categorization: The process of organizing information into distinct groups or classes, one of the fundamental ways both humans and AI structure information.

Concept: A flexible, distributed pattern of knowledge that includes variations and degrees rather than strict definitions.

Concept Distribution: The statistical spread of examples and variations that define a concept's boundaries and typical cases.

Concept Stretching: An educational approach that develops deeper understanding by exploring how concepts manifest across different contexts and domains.

Confusion Matrix: A table used to analyze classification performance, showing correct and incorrect predictions across different categories.

Deep Learning: A method for training deep neural networks that enables them to learn complex patterns from examples.

Deep Neural Network (or Net): A neural network with many layers between input and output, allowing it to learn increasingly complex patterns.

Distributed Processing: Information processing that occurs across many simple connected elements rather than in a central location.

Embedding: The process of converting words or other discrete information into numerical patterns that preserve their relationships and meaning for AI processing.

Expert System: Early AI systems that used explicit rules to make decisions, now largely replaced by neural networks.

Exploitation: In learning systems, the use of currently known successful strategies rather than exploring new possibilities.

Exploration: In learning systems, the trying of new approaches rather than relying on known strategies.

Few-Shot Learning: The ability to learn new tasks or concepts from just a few examples, building on prior learned concepts.

Generative AI (GenAI): AI systems that can create new content (text, images, code, etc.) rather than just analyzing existing information.

Hallucination: When AI generates false or unsupported information while appearing confident in its response.

Interpretability: The degree to which AI internal decision-making processes can be understood by humans.

Knowledge Graph: A structured network showing relationships between pieces of information, often used to supplement neural network processing.

Large Language Model (LLM): An AI system trained on vast amounts of text that can generate human-like language and perform various language-related tasks.

Machine Learning: The process by which AI systems improve their performance through experience, typically by analyzing patterns in data examples rather than explicitly programmed rules.

Meta-Principle: A fundamental concept or approach that applies across many different domains and situations.

Model Collapse: Potential degradation of AI performance when trained primarily on its own outputs rather than original source material.

(Output) Noise: Random variation in AI outputs that isn't systematically biased in any direction.

Optimization: A process of finding the best solution by systematically testing possibilities and adjusting parameters to maximize or minimize a specific metric.

Overfit: When an AI model learns training data patterns too precisely, reducing its ability to generalize to new situations.

Pattern Analysis: Recognizing and processing complex patterns in information.

Patterned Cues: Input patterns that trigger specific responses or activate particular knowledge in AI systems.

Preprocessing: The transformation of raw data into a format suitable for AI processing.

Prompt: The input given to AI that guides its response, including context, examples, and instructions.

Regression: A form of pattern analysis that predicts continuous values rather than discrete categories.

Reinforcement Learning (RL): A type of AI learning where systems learn through trial and error, guided by rewards and penalties.

Reinforcement Learning from Human Feedback (RLHF): A method for fine-tuning AI models based on human preferences and evaluations.

Self-Supervised Learning: Learning approach where the training data itself provides the supervision, without requiring explicit human labeling.

Semi-Supervised Learning: Learning approach where the AI is trained using a small amount of labeled data (with known answers) combined with a larger amount of unlabeled data. This method bridges supervised and unsupervised learning.

Statistical Parrot: A criticism of language models suggesting they only reproduce statistical patterns without true knowledge.

Supervised Learning: Learning from labeled examples where the correct answer is provided during training.

Transfer Learning (AI): Applying knowledge learned in one context to new situations by reusing parts of trained neural networks.

Transformation: The process of converting information from one form or representation to another while preserving meaning.

Unsupervised Learning: Learning that discovers patterns in data without being given correct answers during training.

REFERENCES

Prologue

1   "21st Century Skills." *Wikipedia*. Last modified December 25, 2024. https://en.wikipedia.org/wiki/21st_century_skills.

2   Dasey, T. *Wisdom Factories: AI, Games, and the Education of a Modern Worker*. Massachusetts: Rejuvenate Publishing, 2023.

3   Code.org. "Over 10,000 U.S. High Schools Still Don't Teach Computer Science." *Government Technology*, September 11, 2023. https://www.govtech.com/education/k-12/code-org-over-10-000-high-schools-dont-teach-compsci.

4   Tzanakou, E., R. Michalak, and E. Harth. "The Alopex Process: Visual Receptive Fields by Response Feedback." *Biological Cybernetics* 35, no. 3 (1979): 161–174. https://doi.org/10.1007/BF00337061.

5   Dasey, T. J. *Unsupervised Global Optimization in the Classification of Handwritten Digits and Visual Evoked Potentials*. PhD diss., Rutgers The State University of New Jersey-New Brunswick and University of Medicine and Dentistry of New Jersey, 1991.

6   Defense Advanced Research Projects Agency. (n.d.). *ARPANET*. DARPA. Defense Advanced Research Projects Agency (DARPA). "ARPANET." *DARPA*. Accessed January 20, 2025. https://www.darpa.mil/about-us/timeline/arpanet.

Introduction

7   The Royal Swedish Academy of Sciences. "The Nobel Prize in Physics 2024: Press Release." *Nobel Prize Outreach AB*, October 3, 2024. https://www.nobelprize.org/prizes/physics/2024/press-release/.

8   Miller, K. "From Brain to Machine: The Unexpected Journey of Neural Networks." *Stanford HAI*, November 18, 2024.

https://hai.stanford.edu/news/from-brain-to-machine-the-unexpected-journey-of-neural-networks.

9   Ren, J., and F. Xia. "Brain-Inspired Artificial Intelligence: A Comprehensive Review." *arXiv preprint* arXiv:2408.14811 (2024). https://arxiv.org/html/2408.14811v1.

10 Savage, N. "How AI and Neuroscience Drive Each Other Forwards." *Nature* 571 (2019): S15–S17. https://doi.org/10.1038/d41586-019-02212-4.

11 Richards, B. A., T. P. Lillicrap, S. Beaudoin, *et al.* "A Deep Learning Framework for Neuroscience." *Nature Neuroscience* 22, no. 11 (2019): 1761–1770. https://doi.org/10.1038/s41593-019-0520-2.

12 Chen, Z., and A. Yadollahpour. "A New Era in Cognitive Neuroscience: The Tidal Wave of Artificial Intelligence (AI)." *BMC Neuroscience* 25, no. 23 (2024). https://doi.org/10.1186/s12868-024-00869-w.

13 Lagani, G., F. Falchi, C. Gennaro, and G. Amato. "Spiking Neural Networks and Bio-Inspired Supervised Deep Learning: A Survey." *arXiv preprint* arXiv:2307.16235 (2023). https://arxiv.org/abs/2307.16235.

14 Hiesinger, P. R. *The Self-Assembling Brain: How Neural Networks Grow Smarter*. Princeton, NJ: Princeton University Press, 2021.

15 Dasey, T. *Wisdom Factories: AI, Games, and the Education of a Modern Worker*. Massachusetts: Rejuvenate Publishing, 2023.

Chapter 1. Pattern Analyzing

16 Shortliffe, E. H. "MYCIN: A Knowledge-Based Computer Program Applied to Infectious Diseases." *Proceedings of the Annual Symposium on Computer Applications in Medical Care* (October 5, 1977): 66–69. https://www.ncbi.nlm.nih.gov/pmc/articles/PMC2464549/.

17 Yu, V. L., L. M. Fagan, S. M. Wraith, et al. "Antimicrobial Selection by a Computer: A Blinded Evaluation by Infectious Diseases Experts." *JAMA* 242, no. 12 (1979): 1279–1282. https://doi.org/10.1001/jama.1979.03300120033020.

18 Image from Ronaghan, S. "Deep Learning: Overview of Neurons and Activation Functions." *Medium*, July 2, 2018. Accessed November 4,

2024. https://srnghn.medium.com/deep-learning-overview-of-neurons-and-activation-functions-1d98286cf1e4.

[19] Ju, T., Sun, W., Du, W., Yuan, X., Ren, Z., and Liu, G. "How Large Language Models Encode Context Knowledge? A Layer-Wise Probing Study." *arXiv preprint* arXiv:2402.16061 (2024). https://arxiv.org/abs/2402.16061.

[20] Vig, J., and Y. Belinkov. "Analyzing the Structure of Attention in a Transformer Language Model." In *Proceedings of the 2019 ACL Workshop BlackboxNLP: Analyzing and Interpreting Neural Networks for NLP*, 63–76. Florence, Italy: Association for Computational Linguistics, 2019.

[21] Image formed from a combination of figures in Lee, H., R. Grosse, R. Ranganath, and A. Ng. "Convolutional Deep Belief Networks for Scalable Unsupervised Learning of Hierarchical Representations." In *Proceedings of the 26th International Conference on Machine Learning (ICML 2009)*, 77. New York: Association for Computing Machinery, 2009. https://doi.org/10.1145/1553374.1553453.

[22] Cybenko, G. "Approximation by Superpositions of a Sigmoidal Function." *Mathematics of Control, Signals, and Systems* 2, no. 4 (1989): 303–314. https://doi.org/10.1007/BF02551274.

[23] Schmidhuber, J. "Learning Complex, Extended Sequences Using the Principle of History Compression." *Neural Computation* 4, no. 2 (1992): 234–242. https://doi.org/10.1162/neco.1992.4.2.234.

[24] Goodfellow, I., Y. Bengio, and A. Courville. *Deep Learning*. Cambridge, MA: MIT Press, 2016.

[25] Carandini, M., and D.J. Heeger. "Normalization as a Canonical Neural Computation." *Nature Reviews Neuroscience* 13, no. 1 (2012): 51–62. https://doi.org/10.1038/nrn3136.

[26] LeCun, Y., B. Boser, J. S. Denker, *et. al.* "Backpropagation Applied to Handwritten Zip Code Recognition." *Neural Computation* 1, no. 4 (1989): 541–551. https://doi.org/10.1162/neco.1989.1.4.541.

[27] Hochreiter, S., and J. Schmidhuber. "Long Short-Term Memory." *Neural Computation* 9, no. 8 (1997): 1735–1780. https://doi.org/10.1162/neco.1997.9.8.1735.

[28] Goodfellow, I., J. Pouget-Abadie, M. Mirza, *et al.* "Generative Adversarial Nets." In *Adv in Neural Info Proc Sys*, vol. 27, 2672–2680. 2014. https://arxiv.org/pdf/1406.2661.

29   Vaswani, A., N. Shazeer, N. Parmar, *et al.* "Attention Is All You Need." In *Advances in Neural Information Processing Systems* 30 (2017): 5998–6008. https://papers.nips.cc/paper/7181-attention-is-all-you-need.pdf

30   Dao, T., D. Y. Fu, S. Ermon, A. Rudra, and C. Ré. "FlashAttention: Fast and Memory-Efficient Exact Attention with IO-Awareness." In *Advances in Neural Information Processing Systems* 35 (2022): 16344–16359. https://arxiv.org/pdf/2205.14135.

31   Dhariwal, P., and A. Nichol. "Diffusion Models Beat GANs on Image Synthesis." In *Adv Neural Info Proc Sys* 34 (2021): 8780–8794. https://proceedings.neurips.cc/paper/2021/file/49ad23d1ec9fa4bd8 d77d02681df5cfa-Paper.pdf.

32   Naresh, C., P. S. C. Bose, and C. Rao. "Shape Memory Alloys: A State of Art Review." *IOP Conference Series: Materials Science and Engineering* 149 (2016): 012054. https://doi.org/10.1088/1757-899X/149/1/012054.

33   Chaplin, D. D. "Overview of the Immune Response." *The Journal of Allergy and Clinical Immunology* 125, no. 2 (2010): S3–S23. https://doi.org/10.1016/j.jaci.2009.12.980.

34   Gross, C. G. "Genealogy of the 'Grandmother Cell.'" *Neuroscientist* 8, no. 5 (2002): 512–518. https://doi.org/10.1177/107385802237175.

35   Cook, A. M. "Status Epilepticus." In *Critical Care Self-Assessment Program (CCSAP) 2017 Book 3: Neurocritical Care/Technology in the ICU*. Lenexa, KS: American College of Clinical Pharmacy, 2017. https://www.accp.com/docs/ccsap/CCSAP_2017Book3_Sample_Cha pter.pdf.

36   Nader, K., and O. Hardt. "A Single Standard for Memory: The Case for Reconsolidation." *Nature Reviews Neuroscience* 10, no. 3 (2009): 224–234. https://doi.org/10.1038/nrn2590.

37   Danzig, R. "Machines, Bureaucracies, and Markets as Artificial Intelligences." *Center for Security and Emerging Tech.*, January 2022. https://cset.georgetown.edu/publication/machines-bureaucracies-and-markets-as-artificial-intelligences/.

38   Hayek, F. A. *The Use of Knowledge in Society.* The American Economic Review 35, no. 4 (1945): 519–530.

39   Simon, H. A. *The Sciences of the Artificial.* 3rd ed. Cambridge, MA: MIT Press, 1996.

40   Bicchieri, C. *Norms in the Wild: How to Diagnose, Measure, and Change Social Norms.* New York: Oxford University Press, 2017.

41   Parsons, T. *The Social System.* Glencoe, IL: Free Press, 1951.

42   Smith, V. L. *Rationality in Economics: Constructivist and Ecological Forms.* New York: Cambridge University Press, 2007.

43   Weber, M. *Economy and Society: An Outline of Interpretive Sociology.* Edited by G. Roth and C. Wittich. Berkeley: University of California Press, 1978.

44   Scott, J. C. *Seeing Like a State: How Certain Schemes to Improve the Human Condition Have Failed.* New Haven, CT: Yale University Press, 1999.

45   Harari, Y. N. *Homo Deus: A Brief History of Tomorrow.* New York: HarperCollins, 2017.

46   Blouw, P., E. Solodkin, P. Thagard, and C. Eliasmith. "Concepts as Semantic Pointers: A Framework and Computational Model." *Cognitive Science* 40, no. 5 (2016): 1128–1162. https://www.doi.org/10.1111/cogs.12265.

Chapter 2. Transforming

47   Li, R. S. Yang, D. A. Ross, and A. Kanazawa. "AI Choreographer: Music Conditioned 3D Dance Generation with AIST++." *arXiv preprint* arXiv:2101.08779 (2021). https://arxiv.org/abs/2101.08779.

48   Kreuk, F., G. Synnaeve, A. Polyak, *et al.* "AudioGen: Textually Guided Audio Generation." *arXiv preprint* arXiv:2209.15352 (2022). https://arxiv.org/abs/2209.15352.

49   Anumanchipalli, G. K., Chartier, J., and Chang, E. F. "Speech Synthesis from Neural Decoding of Spoken Sentences." *Nature* 568, no. 7753 (2019): 493–98. https://doi.org/10.1038/s41586-019-1119-1.

50   Laskin, M., L. Wang, J. Oh, E. Parisotto, *et al.* "In-Context Reinforcement Learning with Algorithm Distillation." *arXiv preprint* arXiv:2210.14215 (2022). http://doi.org/10.48550/arXiv.2210.14215.

51   Sher, S., and C. R. M. McKenzie. "Framing Effects and Rationality." In *The Probabilistic Mind: Prospects for Bayesian Cognitive Science,* edited by N. Chater and M. Oaksford, 79-96. Oxford: Oxford University Press, 2008. doi.org/10.1093/acprof:oso/9780199216093.003.0004.

52 Cao, H. "Recent Advances in Text Embedding: A Comprehensive Review of Top-Performing Methods on the MTEB Benchmark." *arXiv preprint* arXiv:2406.01607 (2024). arxiv.org/abs/2406.01607.

53 Ju, X., S. Farrell, P. Calafiura, D. Murnane, et al. "Graph Neural Networks for Particle Reconstruction in High Energy Physics Detectors." *arXiv preprint* arXiv:2003.11603 (2020). https://arxiv.org/abs/2003.11603.

54 Dasey, T. "Detection of AI Cheating: Unreliable and a Distraction." *LinkedIn*, Jan. 16, 2024. https://www.linkedin.com/pulse/detection-ai-cheating-unreliable-distraction-tim-dasey-ph-d--rrobe/.

55 Kaplan, K. A. "Facemash Creator Survives Ad Board." *The Harvard Crimson*, November 19, 2003. Archived May 4, 2019. Accessed December 23, 2024. thecrimson.com/article/2003/11/19/facemash-creator-survives-ad-board-the/.

56 Tversky, A., and Kahneman, D. "Judgment under Uncertainty: Heuristics and Biases." *Science* 185, no. 4157 (1974): 1124–31. https://doi.org/10.1126/science.185.4157.1124.

57 Seghier, M. L. "The Angular Gyrus: Multiple Functions and Multiple Subdivisions." *Neuroscientist* 19, no. 1 (February 2013): 43–61. https://doi.org/10.1177/1073858412440596.

58 Ramsey, R., D. M. Kaplan, and E. S. Cross. "Watch and Learn: The Cognitive Neuroscience of Learning from Others' Actions." *Trends in Neurosciences* 44, no. 6 (2021): 478–491. https://doi.org/10.1016/j.tins.2021.01.007.

Chapter 3. Knowing

59 Plato. *Theaetetus*. Translated by M. J. Levett, revised by M. Burnyeat, and edited by B. Williams. Indianapolis: Hackett Publishing Company, 1992.

60 Gettier, E. L. "Is Justified True Belief Knowledge?" *Analysis* 23, no. 6 (1963): 121–23. https://doi.org/10.1093/analys/23.6.121.

61 Goldman, A. I. "A Causal Theory of Knowing." *The Journal of Philosophy* 64, no. 12 (1967): 357–72. home.csulb.edu/~cwallis/382/readings/Goldmanacausal.pdf.

62 Longino, H. E. *Science as Social Knowledge: Values and Objectivity in Scientific Inquiry*. Princeton: Princeton University Press, 1990.

63   Fricker, M. *Epistemic Injustice: Power and the Ethics of Knowing.* Oxford: Oxford University Press, 2007.

64   Quine, W. V. O. "Epistemology Naturalized." In *Ontological Relativity and Other Essays,* 69–90. New York: Columbia University Press, 1969.

65   Kahneman, D. *Thinking, Fast and Slow.* New York: Farrar, Straus and Giroux, 2011.

66   Aristotle. *Posterior Analytics.* Translated by J. Barnes. Oxford: Clarendon Press, 2002. (Original work published ca. 350 BCE).

67   Aquinas, T. *Summa Theologica.* Translated by the Fathers of the English Dominican Province. New York: Benziger Brothers, 1947. (Original work published ca. 1265–1274).

68   Bloom, B. S., M. D. Engelhart, E. J. Furst, W. H. Hill, and D. R. Krathwohl. *Taxonomy of Educational Objectives: The Classification of Educational Goals. Handbook I: Cognitive Domain.* New York: David McKay Company, 1956.

69   Bruner, J. S. *The Process of Education.* Revised edition. Cambridge, MA: Harvard University Press, 1976.

70   Hutchins, E. *Cognition in the Wild.* Cambridge, MA: MIT Press, 1996.

71   Reber, A. S. "Implicit Learning and Tacit Knowledge." *Journal of Experimental Psychology: General* 118, no. 3 (1989): 219–35. https://doi.org/10.1037/0096-3445.118.3.219.

72   Lieberman, M. D. "Intuition: A Social Cognitive Neuroscience Approach." *Psychological Bulletin* 126, no. 1 (2000): 109–37. https://doi.org/10.1037/0033-2909.126.1.109.

73   Dehaene, S., and J. P. Changeux. "Experimental and Theoretical Approaches to Conscious Processing." *Neuron* 70, no. 2 (2011): 200–27. https://doi.org/10.1016/j.neuron.2011.03.018.

74   Searle, J. R. "Minds, Brains, and Programs." *Behavioral and Brain Sciences* 3, no. 3 (1980): 417–24. https://www.doi.org/10.1017/S0140525X00005756.

75   Pressman, A. "How a Couple of Olin College Students Helped Spark the AI Chatbot Revolution." *Boston Globe,* June 10, 2023. https://www.bostonglobe.com/2023/06/10/business/how-couple-olin-college-students-helped-spark-ai-chatbot-revolution/.

76   Radford, A., R. Jozefowicz, and I. Sutskever. "Learning to Generate Reviews and Discovering Sentiment." *arXiv preprint* arXiv:1704.01444 (2017). https://arxiv.org/abs/1704.01444.

77   *Ibid*

78   Metz, C. "What OpenAI Really Wants." *Wired*, August 1, 2023. https://www.wired.com/story/what-openai-really-wants/.

79   Yao, D. "SXSW '23: OpenAI Co-Founder Shares the Inside Story of ChatGPT." *AI Business*, March 11, 2023. https://aibusiness.com/nlp/sxsw-23-openai-co-founder-shares-the-story-behind-chatgpt.

80   Pressman, A. "How a Couple of Olin College Students Helped Spark the AI Chatbot Revolution." *Boston Globe*, June 10, 2023. https://www.bostonglobe.com/2023/06/10/business/how-couple-olin-college-students-helped-spark-ai-chatbot-revolution/.

81   Vaswani, A., N. Shazeer, N. Parmar, J. Uszkoreit, *et al.* "Attention Is All You Need." In *Advances in Neural Information Processing Systems* 30 (2017): 5998–6008. https://papers.nips.cc/paper/7181-attention-is-all-you-need.pdf.

82   Anthropic. "Mapping the Mind of a Language Model." *Anthropic*. https://www.anthropic.com/research/mapping-mind-language-model.

83   *Ibid*

84   Hawkins, B. "Golden Gate Claude: What Is It?" Begins With AI, May 24, 2024. https://beginswithai.com/golden-gate-claude/.

85   Templeton, A., T. Conerly, J. Marcus, J. Lindsey, T. Bricken, et al. "Scaling Monosemanticity: Extracting Interpretable Features from Claude 3 Sonnet." *Anthropic*. May 21, 2024. https://transformer-circuits.pub/2024/scaling-monosemanticity/index.html.

86   Bender, E. M., T. Gebru, A. McMillan-Major, and M. Shmitchell. "On the Dangers of Stochastic Parrots: Can Language Models Be Too Big?" In *Proceedings of the 2021 ACM Conference on Fairness, Accountability, and Transparency*, 610–623. 2021. https://dl.acm.org/doi/10.1145/3442188.3445922.

87   Kahil, N. "ChatGPT's Winter Slumber: Is AI Going on Holiday Mode?" *Wired Middle East*, October 16, 2023. https://wired.me/technology/chatgpts-winter-slumber-is-ai-going-on-holiday-mode/.

Chapter 4. Conceptual

[88]   Kejriwal, M. "Knowledge Graphs: A Practical Review of the Research Landscape." *Information* 13, no. 4 (2022): 161. https://doi.org/10.3390/info13040161.

[89]   Dasey, T. "AI Can Help Durable Skill Through Concept Stretching." *LinkedIn*, September 16, 2024. https://www.linkedin.com/pulse/ai-can-help-durable-skill-through-concept-stretching-tim-dasey-ph-d--dt7re/.

[90]   Dasey, T. "Wise Up to What's Most Important in a Career: Concept Stretching for Adaptability." *Sweet GrAIpes* (Substack), September 16, 2024. https://substack.com/home/post/p-148919145.

[91]   Dasey, T. "Concept Stretching: Bridging Subjects with AI." *Fobizz* Micro lesson, Accessed December 23, 2024. https://plattform.fobizz.com/fortbildungen/1768-concept-stretching-bridging-subjects-with-ai.

[92]   Tversky, A., and D. Kahneman. "Judgment under Uncertainty: Heuristics and Biases." *Science* 185, no. 4157 (1974): 1124–31. https://doi.org/10.1126/science.185.4157.1124.

Chapter 5. Creative

[93]   Hoogman, M., M. Stolte, M. Baas, and E. Kroesbergen. "Creativity and ADHD: A Review of Behavioral Studies, the Effect of Psychostimulants and Neural Underpinnings." *Neuroscience & Biobehavioral Reviews* 119 (2020): 66-85. https://doi.org/10.1016/j.neubiorev.2020.09.029.

[94]   Montuori, A., and R. E. Purser. "Deconstructing the Lone Genius Myth: Toward a Contextual View of Creativity." *Journal of Humanistic Psychology* 35, no. 3 (1995): 69-112. 10.1177/00221678950353005.

[95]   Guzik, E., C. Gilde, and C. Byrge. "The Originality of Machines: AI Takes the Torrance Test." *Journal of Creativity* 1, no. 1 (2023): 15-29. 10.1016/j.yjoc.2023.100065.

[96]   Si, C., D. Yang, and T. Hashimoto. "Can LLMs Generate Novel Research Ideas? A Large-Scale Human Study with 100+ NLP Researchers." *arXiv preprint* arXiv:2409.04109 (2024). arxiv.org/pdf/2409.04109.

97 Chi, M. T. H., P. J. Feltovich, and R. Glaser. "Categorization and Representation of Physics Problems by Experts and Novices." *Cognitive Science* 5, no. 2 (1981): 121–152. https://doi.org/10.1207/s15516709cog0502_2.

98 Kaufman, S. B., and J. C. Kaufman. "Ten Years to Expertise, Many More to Greatness: An Investigation of Modern Writers." *Journal of Creative Behavior* 41, no. 2 (2007): 114–124. https://doi.org/10.1002/j.2162-6057.2007.tb01284.x.

99 Weisberg, R. W. "Creativity and Knowledge: A Challenge to Theories." In *Handbook of Creativity*, edited by Robert J. Sternberg, 226–250. Cambridge: Cambridge University Press, 1999.

100 Cowan, N. *Working Memory Capacity*. New York: Psychology Press, 2006.

101 Smeekens, B. A., and M. J. Kane. "Working Memory Capacity, Mind Wandering, and Creative Cognition: An Individual-Differences Investigation into the Benefits of Controlled Versus Spontaneous Thought." *Psychology of Aesthetics, Creativity, and the Arts* 10, no. 4 (2016): 389–415. https://www.doi.org/10.1037/aca0000046.

102 Tishby, N., and N. Zaslavsky. "Deep Learning and the Information Bottleneck Principle." *2015 IEEE Information Theory Workshop (ITW)*, 2015, 1–5. https://doi.org/10.1109/ITW.2015.7133169.

103 Au, W. "High-Stakes Testing and Curricular Control: A Qualitative Metasynthesis." *Educational Researcher* 36, no. 5 (2007): 258–267. https://doi.org/10.3102/0013189X07306523.

104 Ericsson, K. A., and R. Pool. *Peak: Secrets from the New Science of Expertise*. Boston: Houghton Mifflin Harcourt, 2016.

105 Simonton, D. K. "Creative Productivity: A Predictive and Explanatory Model of Career Trajectories and Landmarks." *Psychological Review* 104, no. 1 (1997): 66–89. https://www.doi.org/10.1037/0033-295X.104.1.66.

106 Le Bas, C., R. J. B. Hassane, and A. Cabagnols. "Prolific Inventors: Who Are They and Where Do They Locate? Evidence from a Five Countries US Patenting Data Set." *International Centre for Economic Research Working Paper* No. 14/2010 (2010).

107 Brown, T. *Change by Design: How Design Thinking Transforms Organizations and Inspires Innovation*. New York: Harper Business, 2009.

108 Edwards, K. M., B. Man, and F. Ahmed. "Sketch2Prototype: Rapid Conceptual Design Exploration and Prototyping with Generative AI." *arXiv preprint* arXiv:2405.12985 (2024). https://arxiv.org/abs/2405.12985.

109 Sio, U. N., and T. C. Ormerod. "Does Incubation Enhance Problem Solving? A Meta-Analytic Review." *Psychological Bulletin* 135, no. 1 (2009): 94–120. https://doi.org/10.1037/a0014212.

110 Sweller, J., J. J. G. van Merriënboer, and F. G. W. C. Paas. "Cognitive Architecture and Instructional Design: 20 Years Later." *Educational Psychology Review* 31, no. 2 (2019): 261–292. https://doi.org/10.1007/s10648-019-09465-5.

111 Runco, M. A., and S. R. Acar. "Divergent Thinking as an Indicator of Creative Potential." *Creativity Research Journal* 24, no. 1 (2012): 66–75. https://doi.org/10.1080/10400419.2012.652929.

112 Kozbelt, A., R. A. Beghetto, and M. A. Runco. "Theories of Creativity." In *The Cambridge Handbook of Creativity*, edited by J. C. Kaufman and R. J. Sternberg, 20–47. Cambridge: Cambridge University Press, 2010. https://doi.org/10.1017/CBO9780511763205.004.

113 Guilford, J. P. "Creative Abilities in the Arts." *Psychological Review* 64, no. 2 (1957): 110-118. https://doi.org/10.1037/h0048280.

114 Fleming, L. "Recombinant Uncertainty in Technological Search." *Management Science* 47, no. 1 (2001): 117–132. https://doi.org/10.1287/mnsc.47.1.117.10671.

115 Leung, A. K. Y., W. W. Maddux, A. D. Galinsky, and C. Chiu. "Multicultural Experience Enhances Creativity: The When and How." *American Psychologist* 63, no. 3 (2008): 169–181. https://doi.org/10.1037/0003-066X.63.3.169.

116 Fauconnier, G., and M. Turner. "Conceptual Integration Networks." *Cognitive Science* 22, no. 2 (1998): 133–187. https://doi.org/10.1207/s15516709cog2202_1.

117 Stokes, P. D. *Creativity from Constraints: The Psychology of Breakthrough*. New York: Springer, 2006.

118 Chen, C. "How a Top Chinese AI Model Overcame US Sanctions." *MIT Technology Review*, January 24, 2025. technologyreview.com/2025/01/24/1110526/china-deepseek-top-ai-despite-sanctions/.

[119]   A. Breton, P. Soupault, P. Eluard, *et. al. The Automatic Message, the Magnetic Fields, the Immaculate Conception.* London: Atlas Press, 1998.

[120]   Amabile, T. M. "The Social Psychology of Creativity: A Componential Conceptualization." *Journal of Personality and Social Psychology* 45, no. 2 (1983): 357-376. https://www.doi.org/10.1037/0022-3514.45.2.357.

[121]   Finke, R. A., T. B. Ward, and S. M. Smith. *Creative Cognition: Theory, Research, and Applications.* Cambridge: MIT Press, 1992. https://doi.org/10.7551/mitpress/7722.001.0001.

[122]   Robinson, K., and L. Aronica. *Creative Schools: The Grassroots Revolution That's Transforming Education.* New York: Penguin, 2016.

[123]   R. Root-Bernstein and M. Root-Bernstein. "Artistic Scientists and Scientific Artists: The Link Between Polymathy and Creativity." In *Creativity: From Potential to Realization,* edited by R. J. Sternberg, E. L. Grigorenko, and J. L. Singer, 127-151. Washington, DC: American Psychological Association, 2004. https://doi.org/10.1037/10692-008.

[124]   Stanovich, K. E., and R. F. West. "Individual Differences in Rational Thought." *Journal of Experimental Psychology: General* 127, no. 2 (1998): 161-188. https://doi.org/10.1037/0096-3445.127.2.161.

[125]   Tetlock, P. E. *Expert Political Judgment: How Good Is It? How Can We Know?* Princeton: Princeton University Press, 2005.

[126]   Kahneman, D., and A. Tversky. "On the Psychology of Prediction." *Psychological Review* 80, no. 4 (1973): 237-251. https://doi.org/10.1037/h0034747.

[127]   Stanovich, K. E. *What Intelligence Tests Miss: The Psychology of Rational Thought.* New Haven: Yale University Press, 2009.

[128]   Lord, C. G., M. R. Lepper, and E. Preston. "Considering the Opposite: A Corrective Strategy for Social Judgment." *Journal of Personality and Social Psychology* 47, no. 6 (1984): 1231-1243. https://doi.org/10.1037/0022-3514.47.6.1231.

[129]   Paulus, P. B., and V. R. Brown. "Enhancing Ideational Creativity in Groups: Lessons from Research on Brainstorming." In *Group Creativity: Innovation Through Collaboration,* edited by P. B. Paulus and B. A. Nijstad, 110-136. New York: Oxford University Press, 2003. https://doi.org/10.1093/acprof:oso/9780195147308.003.0006.

130 Kunda, Z. "The Case for Motivated Reasoning." *Psychological Bulletin* 108, no. 3 (1990): 480-498. https://doi.org/10.1037/0033-2909.108.3.480.

131 LeDoux, J. E. *The Emotional Brain: The Mysterious Underpinnings of Emotional Life.* New York: Simon & Schuster, 1996.

132 Dweck, C. S. "Mindsets and Math/Science Achievement." *Carnegie Corporation of New York-Institute for Advanced Study Commission on Mathematics and Science Education.* New York: Carnegie Corporation, 2008.

133 Edmondson, A. C. "Psychological Safety and Learning Behavior in Work Teams." *Administrative Science* Quarterly 44, no. 2 (1999): 350-383. https://doi.org/10.2307/2666999.

134 Simonton, D. K. "Creativity as Blind Variation and Selective Retention: Is the Creative Process Darwinian?" *Psychological Inquiry* 10, no. 4 (1999): 309-328. http://www.jstor.org/stable/1449455.

135 Bowers, K. S., P. Farvolden, and L. Mermigis. "Intuitive Antecedents of Insight." In *The Creative Cognition Approach,* edited by S. M. Smith, T. B. Ward, and R. A. Finke, 27-51. Cambridge: MIT Press, 1995.

136 Ericsson, K. A., and N. Charness. "Expert Performance: Its Structure and Acquisition." *American Psychologist* 49, no. 8 (1994): 725-747. https://doi.org/10.1037/0003-066X.49.8.725.

137 Klein, G. *Sources of Power: How People Make Decisions.* Cambridge: MIT Press, 1998.

138 Beaty, R. E., M. Benedek, P. J. Silvia, and D. L. Schacter. "Creative Cognition and Brain Network Dynamics." *Trends in Cognitive Sciences* 20, no. 2 (2016): 87-95. doi.org/10.1016/j.tics.2015.10.004.

139 Martindale, C., and A. Dailey. "Creativity, Primary Process Cognition and Personality." *Personality and Individual Differences* 20, no. 4 (1996): 409-414.

140 Csikszentmihalyi, M., and K. Sawyer. "Creative Insight: The Social Dimension of a Solitary Moment." In *The Systems Model of Creativity,* edited by M. Csikszentmihalyi, 73-98. Dordrecht: Springer, 2014. https://doi.org/10.1007/978-94-017-9085-7_7.

141 Amabile, T. M. "Social Psychology of Creativity: A Consensual Assessment Technique." *Journal of Personality and Social Psychology* 43, no. 5 (1982): 997-1013. https://www.doi.org/10.1037/0022-3514.43.5.997.

[142]   Baxter Magolda, M. B. "Self-Authorship as the Common Goal of 21st-Century Education." In *Learning Partnerships: Theory and Models of Practice to Educate for Self-Authorship*, edited by M. B. Baxter Magolda and P. M. King, 1-35. Sterling: Stylus Publishing, 2004. https://doi.org/10.1002/tl.266.

[143]   Sawyer, R. K. *Explaining Creativity: The Science of Human Innovation*. 2nd ed. New York: Oxford University Press, 2012.

[144]   Gokaslan, A. *et al.* CommonCanvas: An Open Diffusion Model Trained with Creative-Commons Images", *arXiv* preprint arXiv:2310.16825 (2023). https://doi.org/10.48550/arXiv.2310.16825.

[145]   Ecekamar. "Introducing Phi-4: Microsoft's Newest Small Language Model Specializing in Complex Reasoning." *Microsoft*, December 13, 2024. techcommunity.microsoft.com/blog/aiplatformblog/introducing-phi-4-microsoft%e2%80%99s-newest-small-language-model-specializing-in-comple/4357090.

Chapter 6. Learning

[146]   Skinner, B. F. *The Technology of Teaching*. New York: Appleton-Century-Crofts, 1968.

[147]   The concept of backpropagation was developed in Werbos, P. J. *Beyond Regression: New Tools for Prediction and Analysis in the Behavioral Sciences*. Doctoral dissertation, Harvard University, 1974. His dissertation was largely overlooked. The concept was reinvented and coined backpropagation in Rumelhart, D. E., G. E. Hinton, and R. J. Williams. "Learning Representations by Back-Propagating Errors." *Nature* 323, no. 6088 (1986): 533–536. doi.org/10.1038/323533a0.

[148]   Hinton, G. E., S. Osindero, and Y.-W. Teh. "A Fast Learning Algorithm for Deep Belief Nets." Neural *Computation* 18, no. 7 (2006): 1527–1554. https://doi.org/10.1162/neco.2006.18.7.1527.

[149]   Krizhevsky, A., I. Sutskever, and G. E. Hinton. "ImageNet Classification with Deep Convolutional Neural Networks." *Advances in Neural Information Processing Systems* 25 (2012): 1097–1105. https://doi.org/10.1145/3065386.

[150]   Goodfellow, I., Y. Bengio, and A. Courville. *Deep Learning*. Cambridge, MA: MIT Press, 2016.

[151] Srivastava, N., G. Hinton, A. Krizhevsky, I. Sutskever, and R. Salakhutdinov. "Dropout: A Simple Way to Prevent Neural Networks from Overfitting." *Journal of Machine Learning Research* 15 (2014): 1929–1958.

[152] Han, S., J. Pool, J. Tran, and W. Dally. "Learning Both Weights and Connections for Efficient Neural Networks." In *Advances in Neural Information Processing Systems* – Volume 1 (NIPS '15). MIT Press, Cambridge, MA, USA (2015): 1135–1143.

[153] Kingma, D. P., and J. Ba. "Adam: A Method for Stochastic Optimization." In *Proceedings of the 3rd International Conference on Learning Representations* (2015). doi.org/10.48550/arXiv.1412.6980.

[154] He, K., X. Zhang, S. Ren, and J. Sun. "Deep Residual Learning for Image Recognition." In *Proceedings of the IEEE Conference on Computer Vision and Pattern Recognition (CVPR)*, 770–778, 2016. https://doi.org/10.1109/CVPR.2016.90.

[155] Kleinman, Z., and C. Vallance. "AI 'Godfather' Geoffrey Hinton Warns of Dangers as He Quits Google." *BBC News.* May 2, 2023. https://www.bbc.com/news/world-us-canada-65452940.

[156] Senior, A. W., et al. "Improved Protein Structure Prediction Using Potentials from Deep Learning." *Nature* 577, no. 7792 (2020): 706–710. https://doi.org/10.1038/s41586-019-1923-7.

[157] The Nobel Prize. "The Nobel Prize in Chemistry 2024." Press Release. Oct. 2024. https://www.nobelprize.org/prizes/chemistry/2024/press-release/.

[158] Winkler, J. K., C. Fink, F. Toberer, *et al.* "Association Between Surgical Skin Markings in Dermoscopic Images and Diagnostic Performance of a Deep Learning Convolutional Neural Network for Melanoma Recognition." *JAMA Dermatology* 155, no. 10 (2019): 1135–1141. https://doi.org/10.1001/jamadermatol.2019.1735.

[159] OpenAI. "Faulty Reward Functions in the Wild." *OpenAI Blog.* December 14, 2016. https://openai.com/index/faulty-reward-functions/.

[160] Shumailov, I., Shumaylov, Z., Zhao, Y. *et al.* AI models collapse when trained on recursively generated data. *Nature* 631, 755–759 (2024). https://doi.org/10.1038/s41586-024-07566-y.

Chapter 7. Adaptive

[161] Niv, Y. "Reinforcement Learning in the Brain." *Journal of Mathematical Psychology* 53, no. 3 (2009): 139–154. https://doi.org/10.1016/j.jmp.2008.12.005.

[162] Silver, D., A. Huang, C. J. Maddison, A. Guez, L. Sifre, G. van den Driessche, et al. "Mastering the Game of Go with Deep Neural Networks and Tree Search." *Nature* 529 (2016): 484–489. https://doi.org/10.1038/nature16961.

[163] Sun, C., H. Qian, and C. Miao. "From Psychological Curiosity to Artificial Curiosity: Curiosity-Driven Learning in Artificial Intelligence Tasks." *arXiv*, 2022. https://arxiv.org/pdf/2201.08300.

[164] Sutton, R. S., and A. G. Barto. *Reinforcement Learning: An Introduction*. 2nd ed. Cambridge, MA: MIT Press, 2018.

[165] Skinner, B. F. "The science of learning and the art of teaching." *Harvard Educational Review* 24 (1954): 86-97.

[166] Piaget, J. *The Science of Education and the Psychology of the Child*. New York: Viking Press, 1970.

[167] Nakkiran, P. "Learning Rate Annealing Can Provably Help Generalization, Even for Convex Problems." *arXiv*, May 15, 2020. https://arxiv.org/abs/2005.07360.

[168] Barto, A. G., and S. Mahadevan. "Recent Advances in Hierarchical Reinforcement Learning." *Discrete Event Dynamic Systems* 13, no. 4 (2003): 341–379. https://doi.org/10.1023/A:1022140919877.

[169] Christiano, P. F., J. Leike, T. Brown, M. Martic, S. Legg, and D. Amodei. "Deep Reinforcement Learning from Human Preferences." In *Advances in Neural Information Processing Systems* 30 (2017): 4299–4307.

[170] DeepSeek-AI et al. "DeepSeek-R1: Incentivizing Reasoning Capability in LLMs via Reinforcement Learning." *arXiv*, 22 Jan. 2025, https://arxiv.org/abs/2501.12948.

[171] *Ibid.*

[172] Felleman, D. J., and D. C. Van Essen. "Distributed Hierarchical Processing in the Primate Cerebral Cortex." *Cerebral Cortex* 1, no. 1 (1991): 1–47. https://doi.org/10.1093/cercor/1.1.1-a.

173 Doya, K. "What Are the Computations of the Cerebellum, the Basal Ganglia and the Cerebral Cortex?" *Neural Networks* 12, no. 7–8 (1999): 961–974. https://doi.org/10.1016/S0893-6080(99)00046-5.

174 Merzenich, M. M., J. H. Kaas, J. T. Wall, R. J. Nelson, M. Sur, and D. J. Felleman. "Topographic Reorganization of Somatosensory Cortical Areas 3b and 1 in Adult Monkeys Following Restricted Deafferentation." *Neuroscience* 8, no. 1 (1983): 33–55. https://doi.org/10.1016/0306-4522(83)90024-6.

175 Herzfeld, D. J., Y. Kojima, R. Soetedjo, and R. Shadmehr. Encoding of error and learning to correct that error by the Purkinje cells of the cerebellum. *Nat Neurosci.* 2018 May;21(5):736-743.

176 Kuriyama, R., H. Yoshimura, and T. Yamazaki. "A Theory of Cerebellar Learning as a Spike-Based Reinforcement Learning in Continuous Time and Space." *bioRxiv* (2024). https://doi.org/10.1101/2024.06.23.600300.

177 Schultz, W., P. Dayan, and P. R. Montague. "A Neural Substrate of Prediction and Reward." *Science* 275, no. 5306 (1997): 1593–1599. https://doi.org/10.1126/science.275.5306.1593.

Chapter 8. Data-Driven

178 Hoel, E. P. "The Overfitted Brain: Dreams Evolved to Assist Generalization." *Patterns* 2, no. 5 (2021): 100244. https://doi.org/10.1016/j.patter.2021.100244.

179 I. Shumailov, Z. Shumaylov, Y. Zhao, N. Papernot, R. Anderson, and Y. Gal. "AI Models Collapse When Trained on Recursively Generated Data." *Nature* 631 (2024): 755–759. doi.org/10.1038/s41586-024-07566-y.

180 Kaur, P., Taghavi, S., Tian, Z., and W. Shi. "A Survey on Simulators for Testing Self-Driving Cars." *arXiv* preprint arXiv:2101.05337 (2021). https://doi.org/10.48550/arXiv.2101.05337.

181 M. Gerstgrasser, R. Schaeffer, A. Dey, R. Rafailov, *et al.* "Is Model Collapse Inevitable? Breaking the Curse of Recursion by Accumulating Real and Synthetic Data." *arXiv* preprint arXiv:2404.01413 (2024). https://arxiv.org/abs/2404.01413.

182 Kolb, D. Experiential Learning: Experience as the Source of Learning and Development. Englewood Cliffs, NJ: Prentice-Hall, 1984.

[183] Zhuang, F., Z. Qi, K. Duan, D. Xi, *et al.* "A Comprehensive Survey on Transfer Learning." *arXiv preprint* arXiv:1911.02685 (2019). https://arxiv.org/abs/1911.02685.

Chapter 9. Erring

[184] Cambridge University Press & Assessment. "'Hallucinate' Is Cambridge Dictionary's Word of the Year 2023." *Cambridge University Press & Assessment*, November 6, 2023. https://www.cambridge.org/news-and-insights/hallucinate-is-cambridge-word-of-the-year-2023.

[185] Huang, L., W. Yu, and W. Ma, et al. "A Survey on Hallucination in Large Language Models: Principles, Taxonomy, Challenges, and Open Questions." *ACM Transactions on Information Systems* 43, no. 2 (2025): 1–55. https://doi.org/10.1145/3703155.

[186] Chaudhari, S., P. Aggarwal, V. Murahari, *et al.* "RLHF Deciphered: A Critical Analysis of Reinforcement Learning from Human Feedback for LLMs." *arXiv preprint* arXiv:2404.08555 (2024). https://arxiv.org/abs/2404.08555.

[187] DataCamp. "What Is Prompt Injection? Types of Attacks & Defenses." *DataCamp*, July 24, 2024. https://www.datacamp.com/blog/prompt-injection-attack.

[188] Yu, J., Wu, Y., Shu, D., Jin, M., and Xing, X. "Assessing Prompt Injection Risks in 200+ Custom GPTs." *arXiv preprint* arXiv:2311.11538, 2023 (rev. 2024). https://arxiv.org/abs/2311.11538.

[189] A. Hussain, M. R. I. Rabin, T. Ahmed, B. Xu, P. Devanbu, and M. A. Alipour. "Trojans in Large Language Models of Code: A Critical Review through a Trigger-Based Taxonomy," *arXiv*, May 5, 2024, https://doi.org/10.48550/arXiv.2405.02828.

[190] Pasquini, D., M. Strohmeier, and C. Troncoso. "Neural Exec: Learning (and Learning from) Execution Triggers for Prompt Injection Attacks." *arXiv* preprint arXiv:2403.03792v2, March 2, 2024. arxiv.org/pdf/2403.03792.

[191] Arcesati, R. "China's AI Development Model in an Era of Technological Deglobalization," *Institute on Global Conflict and Cooperation (IGCC) and Mercator Institute for China Studies (MERICS)*, April 2024, https://merics.org/sites/default/files/2024-05/Arcesati-China%20AI%20Development-04.25.24.pdf.

192 Zhang, M. "Google Photos Tags Two African Americans as 'Gorillas' Through Facial Recognition Software." *Forbes*, July 1, 2015. https://www.forbes.com/sites/mzhang/2015/07/01/google-photos-tags-two-african-americans-as-gorillas-through-facial-recognition-software/?sh=37d1a37e713d.

193 Grant, N., and Hill, K. "Google's Photo App Still Can't Find Gorillas. And Neither Can Apple's." The New York Times, May 22, 2023. https://www.nytimes.com/2023/05/22/technology/ai-photo-labels-google-apple.html.

194 Kahneman, D. *Thinking, Fast and Slow*. New York: Farrar, Straus and Giroux, 2011.

195 Ramji-Nogales, J., Schoenholtz, A. I., and Schrag, P. G. "Refugee Roulette: Disparities in Asylum Adjudication." *Stanford Law Review* 60 (2007): 295–412. https://scholarship.law.georgetown.edu/cgi/viewcontent.cgi?article=2914&context=facpub.

196 BBC News. "Google Apologises for Photos App's Racist Blunder." *BBC News*, July 1, 2015. https://www.bbc.com/news/technology-33347866.

197 Zhang, M. "Google Photos Tags Two African Americans as 'Gorillas' Through Facial Recognition Software." *Forbes*, July 1, 2015. https://www.forbes.com/sites/mzhang/2015/07/01/google-photos-tags-two-african-americans-as-gorillas-through-facial-recognition-software/?sh=13aa458b713d.

198 Grant, N., and Hill, K. "Google's Photo App Still Can't Find Gorillas. And Neither Can Apple's." *The New York Times*, May 22, 2023. https://www.nytimes.com/2023/05/22/technology/ai-photo-labels-google-apple.html.

199 Wang, X., Wei, J., Schuurmans, D., Le, Q., Chi, E., Narang, S., et al. "Self-Consistency Improves Chain of Thought Reasoning in Language Models." arXiv preprint arXiv:2203.11171 (2022). https://arxiv.org/abs/2203.11171.

200 Henrich, J., S. J. Heine, and A. Norenzayan. "The Weirdest People in the World?" *Behavioral and Brain Sciences* 33, no. 2–3 (2010): 61–83. https://doi.org/10.1017/S0140525X0999152X.

201 Pillay, T. "AI Models Are Getting Smarter. New Tests Are Racing to Catch Up." *Time*, December 24, 2024. https://time.com/7203729/ai-evaluations-safety/.

202   Goh, E., R. Gallo, J. Hom, E Strong, Y. Weng, *et al.* "Large Language Model Influence on Diagnostic Reasoning: A Randomized Clinical Trial." *JAMA Network Open* 7, no. 10 (2024): e2440969. doi.org/10.1001/jamanetworkopen.2024.40969.

Getting Started

203   Martinez, S. L., and G. S. Stager. *Invent to Learn: Making, Tinkering, and Engineering in the Classroom.* 2nd ed. Torrance, CA: Constructing Modern Knowledge Press, 2019.

204   Open Science Collaboration. "Estimating the Reproducibility of Psychological Science." *Science* 349, no. 6251 (2015): aac4716. https://doi.org/10.1126/science.aac4716.

205   Perry, T., R. Morris, and R. Lea. "A Decade of Replication Study in Education? A Mapping Review (2011–2020)." *Educational Research and Evaluation* 27, no. 1–2 (2022): 12–34.

206   Makel, M. C., and J. A. Plucker. "Facts Are More Important Than Novelty: Replication in the Education Sciences." *Ed Res* 43, no. 6 (2014): 304-316. doi.org/10.3102/0013189X14545513

207   Patall, E. A., H. Cooper, and A. S. Wynn. "The Effectiveness and Relative Importance of Choice in the Classroom." *Journal of Educational Psychology* 102, no. 4 (2010): 896–915. https://doi.org/10.1037/a0019545.

208   Pan, S. C., and S. K. Carpenter. "Prequestioning and Pretesting Effects: A Review of Empirical Research, Theoretical Perspectives, and Implications for Educational Practice." *Educational Psychology Review* 35 (2023): 97. https://doi.org/10.1007/s10648-023-09814-5.

209   Kapur, M. *Productive Failure: Unlocking Deeper Learning Through the Science of Failing.* Hoboken, NJ: Wiley, 2023.

210   Kolb, D. A. *Experiential Learning: Experience as the Source of Learning and Development.* 2nd ed. Upper Saddle River, NJ: Pearson Education, 2015.

211   Dasey, T. "Be Careful of Stealing a Student's Realizations, Especially with AI Training." *Sweet GrAIpes* (Substack), March 10, 2024. https://timdasey.substack.com/p/be-careful-of-stealing-a-students.

212   Braithwaite, D. W., and R. L. Goldstone. "Effects of Variation and Prior Knowledge on Abstract Concept Learning." *Cognition and Instruction* 33, no. 3 (2015): 226–256. doi.org/10.1080/07370008.2015.1067215.

213   Pintrich, P. R. "The Role of Metacognitive Knowledge in Learning, Teaching, and Assessing." *Theory Into Practice* 41, no. 4 (2002): 219–225. https://doi.org/10.1207/s15430421tip4104_3.

214   National Research Council. *How People Learn: Brain, Mind, Experience, and School.* Washington, DC: The National Academy Press, 2000. https://doi.org/10.17226/9853.

215   Eseryel, D., V. Law, D. Ifenthaler, X. Ge, and R. Miller. "An Investigation of the Interrelationships between Motivation, Engagement, and Complex Problem Solving in Game-based Learning." *Educational Technology & Society* 17, no. 1 (2014): 42-53.

216   Dingsøyr, T., S. Nerur, V. Balijepally, and N. B. Moe. "A Decade of Agile Methodologies: Towards Explaining Agile Software Development." *Journal of Systems and Software* 85, no. 6 (2012): 1213-1221. https://doi.org/10.1016/j.jss.2012.02.033.

What's Next

217   Kaplan, J., S. McCandlish, T. Henighan, T. B. Brown, *et al.* "Scaling Laws for Neural Language Models." *arXiv preprint* arXiv:2001.08361 (2020). https://arxiv.org/abs/2001.08361.

218   Roser, M., H. Ritchie, and E. Mathieu. "What is Moore's Law?" *Our World in Data.* March 28, 2023. Accessed December 27, 2024. https://ourworldindata.org/moores-law.

219   G., Katja, J. Salvatier, A. Dafoe, B. Zhang, and O. Evans. "When Will AI Exceed Human Performance? Evidence from AI Experts." *Journal of Artificial Intelligence Research* 62 (2018): 729-754. https://doi.org/10.1613/jair.1.11222.

220   DevelopersIndia. "OpenAI o3 Is 2727 on Codeforces, Which Is in the Top 175 of Human Competitive Coders Globally." *Reddit,* Dec. 18, 2024. reddit.com/r/developersIndia/comments/1hiqwko/openai_o3_is_27 27_on_codeforces_which_is/.

221   D. Dai et al. "DeepSeekMoE: Towards Ultimate Expert Specialization in Mixture-of-Experts Language Models." *arXiv,* 11 Jan. 2024, https://doi.org/10.48550/arXiv.2401.06066.

INDEX

www.ingramcontent.com/pod-product-compliance
Lightning Source LLC
Chambersburg PA
CBHW071715120626
46550CB00001B/243